THE
WORLD BOOK
OF

STUDY POWER

THE
WORLD BOOK
OF

STUDY POWER

Volume
1
Learning

STAFF

Publisher Emeritus
William H. Nault

President
John E. Frere

**Vice President,
Editorial Director**
Michael Ross

EDITORIAL

Managing Editor
Maureen Mostyn Liebenson

Associate Editor
Lisa A. Klobuchar

Senior Editor
Mary Feely

Permissions Editor
Janet T. Peterson

Director of Research
Mary Norton

Researcher
Kristina Vaicikonis

Consultants
Thomas H. Estes
Professor of Education
Director of Studies in Reading
 to Learn
McGuffey Reading Center
University of Virginia

Ruth Ravid
Department Chair,
 Foundations and Research
National-Louis University,
 National College of Education

ART

Executive Director
Roberta Dimmer

Art Director
Wilma Stevens

Senior Editorial Artist
Lisa Buckley

Designer
Sandy Newell

Illustrator
Donald Gates

Production Artist
Kelly Shea Doherty

PRODUCT PRODUCTION

**Vice President, Production
and Technology**
Daniel N. Bach

**Director,
Manufacturing/Pre-Press**
Sandra Van den Broucke

Manufacturing Manager
Carma Fazio

**Manufacturing Production
Assistant**
Trisha Ripp

Production Manager
Randi Park

Proofreaders
Anne Dillon
Daniel J. Marotta

PRODUCT DEVELOPMENT

Director
Paul A. Kobasa

Manager
Amy Moses

1996 Printing

©1994 World Book, Inc. All rights reserved. This volume may not be reproduced
in whole or in part in any form without prior written permission from the publisher.

World Book, Inc.
525 W. Monroe
Chicago, IL 60661

ISBN 0-7166-3594-1
Library of Congress Catalog Card No. 93-61400
Printed in the United States of America
 3 4 5 6 7 8 9 10 99 98 97 96

STUDY POWER CONTENTS
VOLUME 1: LEARNING

QUOTES

"A mind stretched to a new idea never goes back to its original dimension."

Oliver Wendell Holmes

CHAPTER

1

A WORLD OF LEARNING

✎ Learning   ✎ Steps to learning

✎ Your route to learning   ✎ Using this book

✎ Lifelong learning   ✎ Parents as teachers

What do you think of when you hear the word "study"? Do you think of a task imposed by a teacher, a parent, or a boss? Do you think, "That's what I have to do to get good grades or prepare for a presentation"? Often, it may seem as though studying is something you do for others, not yourself.

Have you ever spent hours reading, taking notes, seeking out information, and listening to others in order to complete an assignment? And then, having gone through all the motions of studying, did you find that you learned less than you should have? Some people may feel this way even if they perform better than expected.

Learning

Everyone wants to learn and do well. It's human nature to want to take pride in who you are and what you do. Everyone can achieve this sense of pride. Reading this book can help because it explains how you think and learn, and how you can take control of your studying. This is essential, because doing something you want to do feels better than doing something you have to do.

WHY STUDY?

When you have your own reasons for doing something, you're more enthusiastic about it. When your reasons come from others, you may resent having to do the work—and resentment can keep you from doing well.

This book is about understanding yourself so that you can motivate yourself and perform with more confidence at school or work. You'll learn to remove the artificial barrier between studying and learning. When that wall is up, you study because you have to answer to someone else—not because you want the satisfaction of learning. By tearing down the wall, you'll study to learn instead of studying to perform.

Often, if a topic interests you, you call finding out about it "learning." If the topic bores you, you call it "studying," as if studying were distinct from learning. To be effective, studying and learning must come together.

Studying is something people do throughout their lives. As a student, you have assignments to read, papers to write, and tests to take. Studying—even if you're only thinking about studying rather than doing it—is a big part of any student's life.

Studying doesn't end when you leave school. Adults may have oral or written reports to present, budgets to monitor, ideas to evaluate, workshops to attend, and classes to take. To keep up, they need to schedule their time so that they can read and research, listen and write, question and remember. To stay on top of things at work, adults read specialized magazines and journals. To process this deluge of information, they use study skills.

Many people use study skills in everyday life, without even realizing it. For example, suppose you were planning a vacation. What study skills would you use to decide where to go, where to stay, and what to do when you get there? How about when you read maps, planned your travel route, and budgeted for your trip?

If you're not enrolled in school, have you been thinking about going back? Has the thought of studying and taking tests made you put it off? Since you need study skills all your life, regardless of your level of education, you need to know what these skills are, how to use them, and when to use them.

ISN'T STUDYING
FOR STUDENTS?

Knowing how to study effectively will improve your performance—and enjoyment—of school or work and the world.

WHEN DO YOU
STUDY?

Look at the list of study skills that follows. The second and third columns are blank. Fill in the blanks by listing when and how you use these skills.

Study skill	When I use it	How I use it
Remembering details and recognizing how they fit together		
Writing clearly to express what I know		
Reading to understand and remember		
Asking questions to find out or clarify		
Taking notes		
Listening		
Reviewing for tests or presentations		
Taking tests or answering questions		

LEARNING VERSUS
STUDYING

Think about all the things you learned without "studying." You pulled off one of your most amazing feats of learning when you were only a child—you mastered language. In order to communicate, you figured out how to talk.

What else have you learned outside of school? What piqued your curiosity enough to read about it on your own? For example, did you learn more about weather from school or from life? How did you learn about your favorite hobby or sport? Where did you learn about your hometown?

Perhaps one of the most important things you've learned is to ask questions. When you were a young child, most of your communication was in the form of questions. Children are born with an insatiable curiosity. When they start talking, they're full of questions. They wonder why things are the way they are, how things differ, when something happens, where things go, what would happen if . . . ? And they respond to answers with new questions.

But when your world grew larger than your own backyard, you lost this freedom to ask anything anytime. When you were very young, you spent your days with attentive parents, grandparents, siblings, baby sitters, and friends. For most of that time, you enjoyed an adult's undivided attention or were one of a small group. As your world expanded to include first school and later the workplace, you found yourself one among many. The nature of schools and offices makes it impossible for a teacher or a boss to focus on you whenever you have a question. Thus, you had to learn to wait your turn.

This doesn't mean you should stop questioning. Rather, you need to learn when to ask. In school, the day may be broken up into subjects. If a question about science pops into your mind during a social studies class, you need to jot it down and ask it when you get to your science class.

The same is true at the office. If you're in a meeting on a project, your questions about a different assignment will have to wait. It's a matter of knowing when is a good time to ask. To be fair to yourself and others, you should ask your questions at the right time. That way, they'll get the consideration they deserve from the people you're asking.

Questions lead you down the path of learning. They're like green lights telling you to proceed. The road to some answers is a straight line from point A to point B. The road to others is mazelike, with every turn leading you in a different direction as the answers lead you to new questions. When you stop asking, you stop learning.

Questioning is a sign that you're thinking. You're trying to make sense of new information. If it agrees with what you already know, you're likely to accept these new ideas. Simply put, questioning is a way of making the information your own. It becomes more than words in a book or something someone else has said; it's now part of what you know.

HOW DO YOU LEARN?

You learn some things, such as the names of colors, when they are told to you. You can also learn by appreciating or valuing something. Think about a rainbow. A rainbow has seven colors that you can name. But you can learn a great deal more about rainbows by letting your fascination direct you. You can learn science: How are rainbows formed? You can learn folklore: What myths and legends are told to explain rainbows? You can even learn geography and history by studying the different cultures that passed down those myths and legends!

THE SKILLS OF STUDYING

You know that people use study skills to learn, but learning itself takes place inside. In the same way, you can hear someone speak their thoughts, but thinking is internal. Studying is supposed to lead to learning—but as you know, that's not always the case.

When you study, you're trying to make sense of information, whether it's in a book, film, or lecture. Whether you have an assignment to complete or you're simply wondering about something, it's not enough to look at what you are trying to learn. You have to look at yourself as well. What you gain from studying depends on what you bring to the task. Are you willing to study? How well do you manage distractions, such as hunger or noise? How curious are you about the subject you are studying? Your interest—or lack of interest—in a subject may reflect how you were introduced to it. If you don't like a subject, talk to someone who does. Maybe some of that person's enthusiasm can spark your curiosity.

WHY STUDY STUDYING?

This book is a springboard. In it we will explore ways to look at yourself, your assignments, and your approach to studying. This can help you leap over some of the roadblocks to studying well.

When you study, you search for understanding. You read, take notes, listen, and try to remember because you know that you can learn and understand complex ideas, concepts, and subjects. Studying is a means to understanding.

To get the most out of this book, keep the following questions in mind: Why should I study? How do I study? Where should I study? When should I study? What do I need in order to study?

Every time you learn something, you prepare yourself to learn more. For example, you must learn to count before you can learn to add or subtract. And you must learn to add and subtract before you can hope to master more complex mathe-

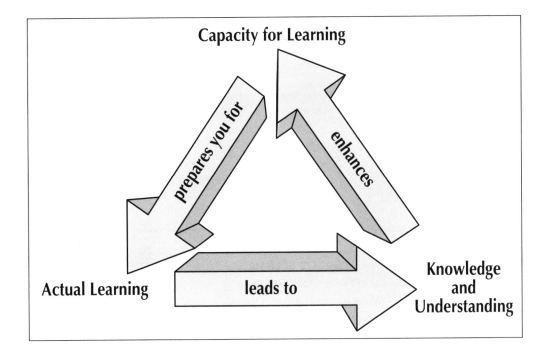

Capacity for Learning

prepares you for

enhances

Actual Learning   **leads to**   **Knowledge and Understanding**

matical principles. The more you learn, the more you are able to learn. That's because by learning something, you expand not only your knowledge but your self-confidence. Every time you complete that circuit, you deepen your understanding of the world.

By studying, you gain control over your own methods of understanding. That may sound odd to you, especially if studying is something you dislike or even dread. But no matter how studying scares or bores you, it is nothing more than a process—a process that lets you climb the steps to learning.

You can use several strategies to accomplish any study task. To study effectively, you must know what strategies you have to choose from, how to use those strategies, and when to use a particular strategy. Students who succeed at school do this instinctively. By making a conscious effort, you too can learn to use a wide range of study strategies.

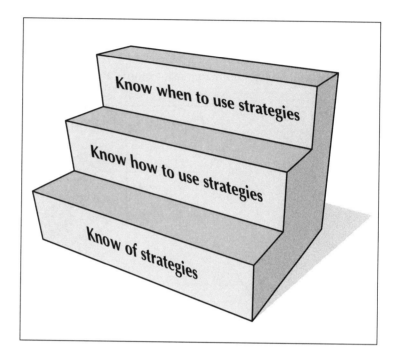

Steps to learning

What happens when you learn something? Your mind changes, but not the way it does when you decide you no longer like your hairstyle. It's a bit more subtle than that.

Learning leads you to new ways of thinking or acting. Because your mind changes, the way you approach things also changes. For example, when Kevin first started borrowing books from the public library, he simply wandered up and down the aisles looking for books he wanted. But after he learned how to use the card catalog and computer search, he could find books he wanted quickly and easily. Now he knows what tools can help him find books, how to use them, and when to use them.

Studying is a process that is supposed to result in learning. Sometimes, however, it doesn't. You may be putting in long hours poring over your textbooks, yet earning only average grades. Or, you may be earning A's but feeling exhausted and overwhelmed.

That doesn't mean you're unable to learn. Rather, it means you need to plan for effective study. Having strategies will put you in control of your learning.

Did you know that the highest achievers aren't necessarily the smartest individuals? Some of the world's most respected thinkers have been poor students. The pioneer in physics, Albert Einstein, failed math. The great inventor Thomas Edison was labeled "addled" by his teacher.

No one today would question the intelligence of these individuals. So why didn't they do well at school? The answer probably lies in the fact that schools then were geared only toward students who learned in a particular way. Students who learned in different ways were seen as failures, no matter how bright they were. Today, some schools continue to teach in a way that suits only some students. These students instinctively know how to master the material covered in class. Others cannot do so until they learn *how* to learn.

What Einstein and Edison did know about themselves—and what you can find out—was how they learned best, what they had to do to reach their goals, what resources they had, and how to get the job done. You can learn to direct your studying so that it pays off. To do so, you must organize your thoughts and time, channel your energy, and connect whatever you're learning to what you already know.

Linking what's already in my brain to new information:
What do I know about this already? How does what I'm reading mesh with what I know already? Does it make it clearer? Does it shed light on ideas I was unsure of? Do I need to replace incorrect details with new ones?

Organizing my thoughts and time:
Do I know what I have to do? Do I know how to reach my goal? What are some ways that I could do this? Of the choices I have, which one is best in this situation? How much time do I have?

Channeling my energy:
Do I monitor internal distractions, such as hunger, fatigue, and emotional highs and lows? What about external distractions, such as noise, lighting, and supplies? What question or questions am I asking?

As you probably realize by now, learning doesn't happen simply because you want it to. Many students believe that learning consists of listening to a teacher and taking notes. But learning takes more effort than that. To truly learn something, you need to prepare yourself. Just as you must warm up before you exercise, you must get ready to learn.

To warm up for learning, you need:

Yourself
What do you know?
What are your strengths?
What are your weaknesses?

What's expected of you, or the criteria
What are you expected to achieve?
How much time do you have to accomplish your task?
How will you be judged or evaluated?
How will you know when you've completed the task?
How will you use what you've learned in the future?

Resources
Who or what will you need to complete the task?
Are teachers, librarians, friends, parents, co-workers, or
    experts in the field on hand to help?
What material resources should you use?
Do you have the equipment and books you need to
    complete the task? If not, can you borrow them?

The task you have to perform
Do you have to prepare a report?
Do you have to pass a test?
Do you have to master a new computer program?
Do you have to give a demonstration?

Strategies
What must you do to successfully complete each task?
Can you break down your task into smaller steps?
How and when can you take those steps?

Involving yourself in learning gives you an edge. If you involve yourself, you size up the work, plan how you're going to do it, decide how to avoid obstacles, and keep tabs on how you're doing. You can create a structure, such as an outline, to help you complete your tasks. You can weigh this against the goals you are working toward and your timetable to make sure you use your energy wisely. By checking your progress, you'll know when and how well you've accomplished your goals.

GIVE YOURSELF AN EDGE

Everybody learns different things in different ways. *How* you learn depends on *what* you learn. You learn how to ride a bike by doing (kinesthetic learning); you learn when bread has been kneaded enough through your hands (tactile learning); you learn to sing, play a musical instrument, or appreciate music by listening (auditory learning); you learn about the movement of the stars and planets by observing (visual learning). Your senses bring all kinds of information to you. Without realizing it, you are learning all kinds of things in all kinds of ways. Usually, if you're learning for your own satisfaction, you instinctively let the task guide you. Without thinking about it, you choose the best way to learn.

DIFFERENT WAYS TO LEARN

Look at learning to operate a computer. Could you do that without actually using a computer? Could you learn phone numbers without memorizing and dialing them? Why do we have science lectures and science labs? Lectures and labs support and reinforce each other. If you didn't have both, you'd miss something.

You can't eat an entire pizza at once—you do it bite by bite. If you take too big a bite, you can choke. It's the same with studying. Break down any task into smaller parts. If you take one bite at a time, you'll be able to enjoy each one.

Your route to learning

Imagine you've come to a fork in a road. The left side of the road is paved. The right side is dirt. You have a choice to make. If you have plenty of time, you might enjoy the scenic route. If you're in a hurry, the highway will get you there on time. Approach studying in the same way. Your choice depends on your needs at the moment. One strategy is better than another only in terms of how well it meets those needs.

YOUR PLAN

Your plan for learning should be based on your strengths or preferences, the resources and time you have, and what's expected of you. Start by asking yourself the following:

- **Why am I trying to learn this?** (I have a report due at the office, I'm memorizing baseball stats because I'm a fan, I want to know the voting record of a certain member of Congress.)

- **How can I make this *my* goal instead of an imposed goal?** (I want to use this computer program to put tables, charts, and graphs in my reports; I want to know more about this sport because all my friends enjoy it; I want to decide whether or not to vote for this person.)

- **What am I bringing to the task?** (I'm bringing what I already know, my experiences, strengths, and weaknesses.)

- **What can I do to meet my goal?** (I can listen to directions or explanations; read books, articles, and reports; watch demonstrations, performances, or videos; write answers or explanations; take notes; draw a map, diagram, or picture; present an oral report or give a lecture; memorize facts, figures, definitions; and ask or answer questions.)

Let's look at a specific task to show how this works. What would you do if you had to learn the spellings and meanings of several words? Maybe you have a vocabulary test coming up. Or maybe you're preparing a report on a new computer system and will use lots of technical words that are new to you. You have a week to review for the test or write the report. You'll be judged on your accuracy.

DEVELOPING A STUDY PLAN

How are you going to stir your own curiosity and drive to learn these words? What attitude can get you through this? This is probably the most difficult step. Maybe you're wondering why you have to do this in the first place. Try to figure out a reason. For example, you could ask yourself, "Why are these words necessary if I don't use them every day?" Perhaps by finding out what the words mean, you may find they become a useful part of your vocabulary.

Now, think about your strengths and weaknesses as a learner. Think about what you should do and what you should avoid doing.

Learning new words involves memorization. If you learn visually, you may want to read the list of words and their definitions. Illustrating the definitions may help. Or, try drawing a box around the word to see what shape the word forms. If you are a verbal learner, you could use the words to make up a story. If you learn best by hearing things, you may want to tape yourself saying, spelling, and defining the word so that you can play it over and over. You could even make up songs about the words. If you learn best by doing, try using the words in everyday conversation. Maybe somebody will ask you what the words mean—that will give you a chance to see if you truly understand them.

Also, think about whether you'll learn better if you work alone or with a companion. Do you like to work at your own pace? Or does another person's enthusiasm help get you going? If another person is working on the same task, you could team up. What size group would be right for you?

Consider what you already know. Which words and spellings already are part of your vocabulary? You don't need to spend time relearning those words. Which words are similar to words you already know? Apply that understanding to the new words.

Which words are completely new? Look them up in a dictionary. Read the definitions and look at the word histories, or etymologies. Finding out where words come from explains a lot about them. Make a conscious effort to connect what you find out to words you already know.

The task is to learn the spelling and definitions of words. Of the strategies mentioned above, which would work best for you? Therein lies your plan.

Where should you work and when? At what time of day do you concentrate best? (Try not to study if you're tired, excited, upset, hungry, or worried—these internal distractions will interfere with your concentration.) Are you more likely to get peace and privacy at a particular time of day?

Does soft background music help you work, or do you require silence? Does too much heat or cold break your concentration? What kind of light do you need—bright or soft? Do you have all the paper, pens, pencils, and books you'll need at your fingertips?

If you try to study for long periods of time, you may feel edgy or find your mind wandering. Give yourself a break. You'll find you'll get more done during your study sessions if you let yourself daydream for a few minutes or get up and stretch. You'll come back to the task with renewed energy and interest. To get perspective on what you're doing, sometimes you need to step back from it.

As you work, check on how you're doing. Is your study plan working for you? Perhaps you came up with a plan and then realized it would take too long to complete. You need to change your plan or pick a new one.

How do you know when you've accomplished your goal? Ask yourself whether you've learned the spellings and definitions. If so, remember the plan you followed, so that you can use it the next time you face a similar task. If not, ask yourself what you should have done differently. Whether or not you've accomplished your goal, ask yourself what tactics you will use again next time and what you will change.

Learning is not simply a matter of luck. It doesn't happen by chance. Learning is the direct result of what you bring to it, how you plan for it, and how you act on that plan.

You have the power to make decisions that affect your success. The best learners are those who can organize their tasks, resources, and study strategies and put them to good use. Successful learning requires knowing yourself, what you have to do, what resources you have, and how you are going to use those resources. Those who study effectively don't necessarily study harder. Successful learners are those who study smarter!

Learning how to learn is a lifelong endeavor. The short-term goals are completing assignments for work or school. The long-term goal is growing in wisdom.

Using this book

This book will help you find ways to make learning interesting. Most people are turned off by rote, dry, or unfruitful learning. No one enjoys any activity that's tedious and futile. Unless you know how to change your approach to learning, the satisfaction of mastering new knowledge may continue to elude you.

It's important that you define your own reasons for using this book. As you read about study strategies and how to apply them, ask yourself which ones suit your learning style. As you learn about smarter ways to search for information, think about how they would have helped on past projects or assignments. Then come up with a few tactics to try as you tackle your next assignment.

Taking control of what you learn will increase your commitment and enjoyment. When your studies lead to learning, your confidence will grow—and with it, your drive to learn.

Here is a description of what this book has to offer you.

1. You'll learn how different students think in different ways. You'll find you have more ways of looking at and solving problems than you previously thought existed. ("Smart Thinking," chapter 2.)

2. You'll see how your initial response to something can either open or close your mind to it. In addition, you'll

learn how to clear barriers that prevent you from finding a reason or time for studying. ("Smart Thinking," chapter 2.)

3. You'll learn what factors can add to or take away from your ability to learn. You'll learn how to manage these factors so that they work in your favor. ("Smart Thinking," chapter 2.)

4. You'll learn to deal with the external and internal distractions that block your concentration. ("Smart Thinking," chapter 2.)

5. You'll find ways to budget your time so that you can learn assigned material and still have time for recreation and relaxation. Spending your time working toward realistic goals will make your studies more inviting. ("Smart Thinking," chapter 2.)

6. You'll learn to create a study plan, using what you know about your strengths, time, resources, and how you will be evaluated. Sometimes, you get locked into one way of doing something, whether it works for you or not. Choosing from different options will let you get things done in a way that suits you. ("Smart Thinking," chapter 2.)

7. You'll take an inventory of your study habits, look at the results, and learn how to play up the habits that work for you and play down those that work against you. Understanding how you can help yourself or get in your own way is an important part of learning. ("Smart Thinking," chapter 2.)

8. You'll become aware of strategies to use when you study, and how and when to use each strategy, so you don't spin your wheels. If you're stuck but continue to do whatever got you stuck, you'll never get moving. On the other hand, if you know of other options, you can experiment with some that may solve the problem. ("Learning Strategies," chapter 3.)

9. You'll learn how to read actively. That way, as you study, you think about whether you understand, and take action as soon as you stop understanding. When

you're actively seeking specific information, connecting what you know with what you read, and seeing how ideas link up, you're organizing your learning so that it's easiest for you to remember. ("Learning Strategies," chapter 3.)

10. You'll learn how to tell the difference between important ideas and trivial ones. This lets you devote your time and energy to those that matter the most. You'll also find it easier to organize information you get from lectures and written materials. ("Learning Strategies," chapter 3.)

11. You'll learn different ways to take notes, so that information is readily available when you need it. This means that you'll be more likely to use your notes, which will help you review for tests or plan and prepare reports. Clear, concise notes can be invaluable as a reminder or a planning tool. ("Learning Strategies," chapter 3.)

12. You'll learn how to expand your vocabulary in a meaningful way instead of through rote memorization. By applying what you already know to new vocabulary, you'll not only understand the dictionary definition of a word more easily, you'll be able to add some personal definitions. Words that mean something to you are easier to learn and use. ("Learning Strategies," chapter 3.)

13. You'll discover where to find information you need. The sheer variety of reference books can make using them seem like more trouble than it's worth. But, if you know the purpose of each type of reference book and where to find it, your research will benefit. ("Resources for Learning," chapter 4.)

14. You'll learn how to tell whether or not a particular resource material will be of use to you. Judging materials before you use them can save you time, energy, and frustration. ("Resources for Learning," chapter 4.)

15. You'll learn how to make the most of the public library, what materials it holds, and how to use them. Librarians are there to help you get the material you

need, even if your library doesn't own a particular source of information. Also, the library offers many time-saving services—you can't take advantage of them if you don't know what they are. ("Resources for Learning," chapter 4.)

16. You'll get tips on using the media and technology as resources. Television, videos, radio, and audiotapes can teach as well as entertain. Learning how to use these sources opens up a new and lively door to learning. ("Resources for Learning," chapter 4.)

17. You'll see how a textbook's organization can help or hinder your learning. Some textbooks are well written, with information that's easy to find and understand. But other textbooks are not. If you're unaware that a poorly written textbook can get in the way of your learning, you may blame yourself for something that's not your fault. With this new knowledge, you can take steps to find sources of meaningful information. ("Resources for Learning," chapter 4.)

18. If you're in school, you'll find ways of solving problems that are unique to students. Uneven workloads or problems at home or with friends can make it hard to do your best. Setbacks are always a part of life, so it's important to learn how to cope with them before you feel overwhelmed. You can ease the tension in healthy, effective ways. ("Where to Turn for Help," chapter 5.)

19. If you're a parent, you'll find ways to support and encourage your children as they try to learn. You may want to talk openly with your children about homework or school, but find that sometimes obstacles crop up. Just as strategies can make studying more effective, they can make communication between you and your children easier, more relaxed, and more helpful. You'll learn when you should offer help and when you should let your child take responsibility. You'll find tips on getting the most out of parent-teacher conferences, and how you can be a partner in your children's education by getting involved at school. ("Learning in the Home," appendix, and "A World of Learning," chapter 1.)

20. If you're a professional, you'll get tips on budgeting your time, handling interruptions, and psyching yourself up for assignments that you'd rather pass on. ("Smart Thinking," chapter 2.)

This book is a map. We hope it will guide you through the territory of learning in an enjoyable and meaningful way. Having a map frees you to explore uncharted territories—to seek out your own ways of enriching your studies.

MAPPING OUT THE TERRITORY

Only you know specifically what you have to do. You must judge the value of any strategy against your strengths, your work, and your goals. You have to decide where a particular strategy might work, and when. You have to decide whether it's right for you. Trust your own instincts. Just because something worked for a friend, sister, or classmate doesn't mean it will work for you.

If you want to extend yourself, wait until you're working on a subject you like—then choose a strategy you wouldn't ordinarily use. Once you become comfortable using the strategy, try applying it to more challenging subjects. Try it the other way around, too. For those assignments that you find most difficult, use the strategies you find easiest.

Lifelong learning

Teachers are found in more places than the classroom. Some of the most important teachers in your life have been members of your family. Take a moment to think about some of the things that you've learned from different relatives. Did your grandfather teach you how to fish? Perhaps your mother taught you a shortcut for doing division problems. Who taught you how to ride a bicycle?

Then, think of what you've learned from friends. Did a friend teach you how to build a tree house or make a model airplane? What games have friends taught you? What ideas have they explained to you?

What have you learned from books, movies, television, computers, or through playing games and participating in sports? How did you learn about people or places in other parts of the world, animals, or how electricity works? How did you learn that leaves change color in the fall? That the moon and planets move? That nights are longer in winter and shorter in the summer?

Now, think of the ways in which you've been your own teacher. What problems have you solved on your own when building something? Did you learn how to read certain words by yourself? It's astounding to realize how much knowledge you can gain simply from interacting with others and the world at large.

YOUR CAPACITY FOR LEARNING

You have an unlimited capacity to learn. However, some things are easier to learn than others, and some ways of learning are easier for you than others. It's easier to learn that a rubber ball bounces than to understand the laws of physics. But once you do learn something, you can use that knowledge to learn something else. You can apply your knowledge of bouncing balls to some principles of physics.

LEARNING AND AGE

The ability to learn has no age limits. You're never too young or too old to learn. Of course, you may be better prepared to learn certain things when you're older. Some concepts are built on many years of experience. For example, your understanding of time is sure to change as you age.

Other concepts are the building blocks. You need to know

how to add before you can multiply. You need to understand how to subtract before you can make change. But even before that, you need to understand what a number is and the value of each number.

Until you understand the basic building blocks, whatever you try to build on a shaky foundation will fall down. Learning is truly easier if you move from understanding to deeper understanding.

It's important that you make the most of what you learn, because learning is truly lifelong. An interesting thing happens when people continue to learn throughout their lives. They remain more active and involved in life.

Your body stops growing after puberty, but your mind can grow throughout your life. Learning is vital to feeling in touch with yourself, your family, your friends, your community, and the world. If you stop learning, your world narrows as you grow older. If you continue to learn, your world is constantly growing, changing, and renewing itself. Your outlook on life won't become tarnished or dulled.

Learning is a hopeful, optimistic endeavor. It may be true that there's nothing new under the sun, but if it's new to you, what does it matter if it's old to someone else?

Parents as teachers

As a parent, you may wonder, "What's the best way to teach children that learning is important?" The answer probably is simpler than you want to think. Without a doubt, the best way for a parent to teach children to value learning is for the parent to be a learner. Children are keen observers. They follow their parents' lead in everything. In their earliest games of pretend, how closely did your children mimic your tone of voice or copy your mannerisms?

Even when they're not pretending, children copy what you do because they want to be like you. They often answer the question, "What do you want to be when you grow up?" by saying, "A dentist, like my mom." As a parent, you are your children's window to the world. You're the one explaining it to them, so they view it as you do.

As they begin seeing more of the world on their own, their questions will show that they're thinking about how things are

done differently at a friend's house, or about the different beliefs or traditions that friends have. In explaining the differences, you impart your family's values.

PASSING ON A
LOVE OF READING

You raise your children to value and respect what you value and respect. If you value and respect learning, your children will as well. To raise readers, you have to be a reader.

Having books and magazines around the house is important, but unless your children see you reading, they won't see the value of reading or experience its joys. When children discuss books with you or overhear you mentioning what you've read, the importance of reading becomes even clearer.

You and your children will learn a great deal about each other when you discuss ideas that come from books. What a wonderful way to find out about how your child perceives things, as well as an opportunity to guide and share.

SHOWING THE
WAY

You've probably noticed that your children have picked up some of your habits that you'd rather not pass on. Although you've said, "You shouldn't do that," your actions send a more powerful message than your words. If you're an enthusiastic person who interrupts others when they speak, how can your children learn to wait their turn to speak?

Instead of focusing on changing your children's behavior, it's better to change your own behavior first. That way, you are showing your child three important things: that your actions and your words send consistent messages; that human beings are flexible and have choices about what they do; and that each individual is responsible for his or her actions and behavior.

"Do as I say, not as I do," is not strong enough. So, if you want your children to be interested in school, you will have to take an interest in their schooling first. It's just like playing follow-the-leader.

When you see your children becoming interested and involved learners, let them know that you notice. Honest praise and encouragement will go a long way. It helped your children when they took their first steps, spoke their first words, and painted their first painting.

CHEERING ON YOUR CHILDREN

When children get older, sometimes we expect them to get things right on the first try. But learning isn't like that. As with any human development, there are things that must come first, mistakes that must be made.

LET CHILDREN MAKE MISTAKES

Your children fell a lot when they were learning to walk, but you taught them to pick themselves up and try again. The same principle applies to learning. Getting close is as important as getting it right—a child can't reach full understanding without first reaching partial understanding.

When your children are learning facts and figures, give them the same freedom to stumble that you gave them when they were learning to walk. If you're always pointing out mistakes or rescuing your children, they won't learn to believe in their abilities.

Solving a problem by dint of your own labor is more satisfying than being told how to do so. That's why children get upset when you show them a solution before they've had time to figure it out themselves. That's why they like to play guessing games and riddles.

Remember, children need to develop at their own pace. You can fertilize the soil and provide the best environment, but you can't make a plant blossom before it is ready. Look at the

example of the bamboo tree. A bamboo shoot grows rapidly from the base of an old tree. The tallest trees grow from the older plants that have stored the most food. The new tree may reach its full height within a few months. Despite this rapid growth, however, the bamboo tree may not bloom for another 30 years.

PRAISE AND EXAMPLE

Learning is more than knowing an answer. It is a process that takes time. Plants need water to thrive, but too much water can kill them. No matter what the neighbors' kids are doing, measure your children's growth by who they are. Giving praise and setting a good example are your most effective methods for nurturing a learner. Look at the following scenarios to see how powerful they are.

Child: I got my history test back today.
Parent: How did you do?
Child: Well . . .
Parent: What do you mean, "Well"? Didn't you get a pretty good grade?
Child puts the paper down and walks away.

Child: I got my history test back today.
Parent: How did you do?
Child: Well . . .
Parent: You sound disappointed, what is it?
Child: I did all right on the first part, but there were all these boxes in the second part, and I knew the answers but I put my answers in the wrong boxes. A machine graded the test so there was no way for the teacher to see that I really got it right.
Parent: That is disappointing. Did you tell your teacher?
Child: No. I figured if I filled in the boxes wrong there would be no point.
Parent: I don't know. I think you ought to show your teacher what happened. Even if he can't change the grade, he can see that you did answer correctly. If he can't change the grade now, he can always use that information at the end of the semester when he's writing up your report card.
Child: I didn't think about it that way. Maybe it would help him to know that those answer keys can mess people up. He did ask me if I wanted to talk about it, but I felt too embarrassed because I thought he was thinking that I didn't review for the test.

The parent in the second example made the child feel more important than the test, listened to what the child had to say, and helped the child decide what to do about the situation. Which child is more likely to feel confident at the next test?

Simply by reading this book, you are showing your child that learning is important. If you know of strategies that can help your children learn, you can remind them to use the strategies when they seem frustrated. You can also be their partner in experimenting with the strategies. Make learning and studying a family habit that you all can enjoy throughout your lives.

A good way to let your child know that education is impor-tant is to become involved at school. Donate whatever time you can to the school. Perhaps it's once a week, perhaps once a month. You could volunteer your time in your child's classes or the library. You could tutor a student who's in need of extra attention. Even if you can manage to get to school only once a year, for example as a chaperon on a field trip, don't hesitate to volunteer. Schools always can use an extra pair of hands.

If you spend time in your child's classroom, the whole class will benefit from the attention an extra adult can provide. You could come as a speaker and talk about a hobby, a special interest, or your career. You could read to the children. You could write down stories for children who cannot yet write fluently themselves. You could hang up bulletin boards. You could show support for the faculty by bringing snacks or flow-ers to the staffroom. Talk to the principal and the teachers to find out how you could help.

If you can't get to the school, perhaps you can donate old toys, books, rugs, or clothes for the kindergarten dress-up or school plays. You could do the children a special favor, such as making tapes of books for them to listen to.

It is very important that you attend special programs at school. Many of these are in the evening so that parents don't have to take time off work. If you are involved in the school, you will be more comfortable talking to teachers about your child, and you will have more confidence in the teachers when you see for yourself all the work that they do.

When it comes time for your parent-teacher conference, you can do some things to get the most out of it and give the teacher more insight into your child. Parent-teacher confer-ences should be a conversation between you and the teacher. Be prepared to give teachers any information that would help them better understand your child. Tell the teachers how you see your child. For example, suppose your child is outgoing at home but shy in crowds. If you tell the teacher this, you can work together to make your child feel more comfortable at school. Tell your child's teachers about your child's likes, dis-likes, and level of confidence and curiosity.

Teachers need to know of any changes at home that might affect your child's behavior or schoolwork. If a relative or pet dies, if you are getting divorced, or if a new baby has recently joined the family, let your child's teachers know. That way, they're more likely to give your child support when he or she needs it.

If you think that your child's grades or work do not reflect his or her intelligence, let the teachers know that as well. Perhaps the teachers are overlooking something about your child's personality or learning style. Get an explanation for anything you don't understand.

If you feel that your child could use extra help or support in school, ask for it. You have to be your child's advocate. If your child has taken standardized tests, ask the teachers to fully explain the results. Ask to see a record of your child's progress through the year, and use this to measure his or her individual growth.

By taking these simple steps, you will show your child that you care about what goes on at school. Your interest will show that school is important, and your child's happiness and progress there matter to you. That, more than anything, can encourage your child's natural yearning for knowledge.

☺ "Tell me, I'll forget. Show me, I may remember. But involve me and I'll understand."

Chinese proverb

CHAPTER

2

SMART
THINKING

✎ Think about thinking   ✎ Types of thinking

✎ Wanting to learn   ✎ Pay attention!

✎ Distractions

To understand how you learn, it helps to look at how your brain works. The brain, after all, is the organ of learning. If you understand how your brain works, you can use that knowledge to make learning easier—just as when you understand how your muscles work, you can tone them and build your strength in the most efficient way.

If you look at a diagram of the brain, you'll see that it has two sides, or hemispheres, that are connected by the corpus callosum. The corpus callosum is a heavy cable of nerves that transmits memories and learning, and allows each half of the brain to communicate with the other.

Think about thinking

Each hemisphere of the brain does part of the complex work of thinking and reasoning. Each works in harmony with the other. You don't feel as though you have two separate minds because the corpus callosum lets the left and right hemispheres of your brain communicate and work together.

If the corpus callosum is damaged, your brain still functions, but you have to compensate for the lack of communication between hemispheres. You have two of many organs, such as eyes, kidneys, and lungs. While life is easier if you can see with both your eyes, for example, you don't need both to survive. You can learn to compensate if you lose your sight in one eye. It's the same with your brain.

Much of what we know about how the brain works comes from studying people whose corpus callosums have been severed for medical reasons; for example, to treat severe seizures. Scientists know a great deal about which part of the brain does what, and how the brain handles each function.

When you perceive, weigh, recognize, or recall information, both hemispheres of your brain are at work. Each does its part in helping you respond to what's going on. When you are cooking, for example, you use one kind of thinking to read the recipe. You use a different kind of thinking to have a hunch that you need less salt than the recipe calls for.

WAYS OF
THINKING

Of course, you may use one part of your brain more than the other when you're doing certain things. When you're folding laundry or balancing your checkbook, the areas that control the recall you need are at work. The same is true if you are drawing or looking at a work of art.

Your brain adapts to handle whatever task you give it. And it does this almost automatically, as if it had a mind of its own! Because much of this is automatic, you don't have to think, "OK, I'm going to read a novel, so I'm going to use this part of my brain but not that part." When you stand up and start walking toward the door, you don't think about shifting your weight to keep your balance—you just do it! At the same time, your brain is constantly judging the distance between the door and you, steering you down the hallway rather than into the walls, and helping you carry on a conversation with a friend. Usually, your brain can handle all these complex tasks—and more—at once, without you even realizing it.

But you have many different ways to think about any particular thing. Sometimes, it's a matter of responding to the options you have. When you're hungry and you open the refrigerator, the foods you see affect your decision about what to eat. Your brain acts in the same way. It has many ways of thinking, so it picks the option that best suits the situation.

Depending on the situation, therefore, your brain may choose a certain type of thought pattern over others. This is true, for example, of emotional experiences. When you're confused, panicky, or elated, your feelings may affect the way you think about and react to a situation. They may seem to block your ability to think at all.

Think about times when your emotions ran high. When you were nervous about an exam, did your mind go completely blank for a minute after you turned over the paper? When you heard noises in the dark, did your mind start replaying every horror movie you'd ever seen, even as you told yourself not to be so silly? When you heard you had received an achievement award, did your mind start racing with so many thoughts that you couldn't grab one? This often happens when people are excited by something or afraid that something will go wrong.

Sometimes, your reactions are more confused. You may meet someone who says and does all the "right" things. You can't think of a logical reason to distrust that person. But you hear a voice in the back of your mind telling you not to trust

HOW YOUR BRAIN REACTS

him or her. Or, you may have gotten lost. Suddenly, you have to decide where to turn next, based on a "feel" for where you want to get to. You don't really "know" which direction is the right one.

In situations like these, you've got to clear your mind and decide what to do next, despite your fear or panic. The same is true when you feel nervous before taking an exam or making a speech. To perform successfully, you have to think clearly in the face of threat. That's the time when you can't rely on your brain's automatic pilot—you have to take over and make a conscious decision.

Types of thinking

Different parts of your brain perceive and interpret information in different ways. One kind of thinking is in play when you act rationally and logically, analyze information, follow steps in directions, plan, keep track of time, or put your thoughts into words. We refer to these types of thinking as "analytic" because when you analyze information, you do so step-by-step, part-to-whole.

The root of the word "analyze" means "to understand by taking apart." If you were programming a computer, building an engine, or conducting a scientific experiment, you'd have to think analytically. Unless you code information into your computer in a specific order, your computer couldn't do what you want. When you put something together, such as a car engine, you must start with the most basic parts and build from there. If you are conducting an experiment, you must do things in a certain order to get the correct result.

But analyzing is only one way in which your brain functions. Other times, you daydream, imagine, or listen to the voice in the back of your head. We think of this as using intuition, acting on a hunch, or getting a message from a "sixth sense."

When you do this, you use intuitive, holistic, and subjective thinking because you're relying on more than meets the eye. When you decide whether to trust someone, how to carve a block of wood into a statue, or which way to turn when you've lost your way, you use this kind of thinking. Improvising songs on the piano or imagining the perfect world in your mind also falls into this category.

When you're lost in these thoughts, time becomes less relevant because you're wrapped up in the experience. These brain functions often are called "global." When you think globally, you synthesize, or combine, information by making parts into a whole. This is the opposite of analyzing, which is breaking down a lot of information into small parts. A fashion designer sketches the outfit before making a pattern. An inventor knows what he or she wants to invent before making the real thing. A sculptor sees a statue in a block of wood.

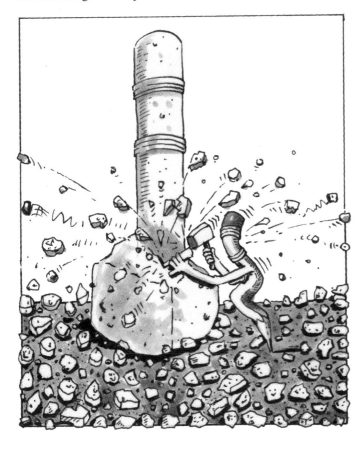

Look at the chart comparing your analytic ways of thinking with your global ways of thinking. You'll notice how varied human thought can be. As you read, think about what you do that falls under each category. This will help you see not just that you can, but that you do indeed use your whole brain!

ANALYTIC VERSUS GLOBAL

Analytic ways of thinking

Verbal—use words to name, define, or describe things (writing a letter, taking part in show and tell)

Symbolic—use symbols that stand for objects or ideas (for example, letters, written words, and numerals) in order to grasp concepts (such as reading, writing, and solving mathematical problems)

Abstract—use a part to represent the whole (speculating about relationships or how things will turn out)

Temporal—remain aware of time, do things in order (making and keeping to schedules, starting to work on a report that's due soon, making sure you have all the ingredients before you start making cookies)

Rational—use reason and facts to draw conclusions (deciding to buy a particular shirt because it is on sale, deciding to take a class because it will look good on your college application)

Digital—use numbers to count and solve problems (balancing a checkbook, measuring, counting how many people are coming to your party so that you can provide enough food)

Logical—use logic and order to draw conclusions (realizing that if all dogs are mammals and if Rufus is a dog, therefore Rufus is a mammal; figuring that if you get sneezing fits every spring, you may be allergic to pollen)

Linear—link ideas or thoughts together in an orderly fashion (writing a traditional outline or programming a computer)

Global ways of thinking

Nonverbal—describe things without using words (drawing and painting, composing music, shrugging instead of saying, "I don't know")

Synthetic—put things together to form something new (inventing new things, finding new uses for things that exist)

Concrete—respond to things as they are at any given moment (acting spontaneously, reading meaning into what someone says or does)

Analogic—recognize similarities between things or ideas that are different (seeing that creationism and evolution are both attempts to explain the diversity of life)

Nontemporal—remain unaware of time or sequence (daydreaming, playing, getting caught up in the moment)

Nonrational—rely on feelings instead of facts to make judgments (reacting to a public service announcement or appeal that plays on emotions, choosing a class that seems interesting over one that would carry more credit)

Spatial—see relationships between things and understand how the parts form the whole (designing a pattern for making a dress)

Intuitive—use hunches, feelings, images, or insight to reach conclusions (acting on impulse, having an answer pop into your mind, choosing a multiple-choice answer because it seems correct)

Holistic—recognize the whole by seeing patterns (figuring out the solution to a mystery story by putting together clues)

When you react to someone or something, what decides which way of thinking you'll use? At times, you'll go with your first response. Other times, you'll want to figure out different approaches. That's because some situations are more complicated than others.

Sometimes, thinking too much about things actually will confuse the situation. You don't need to weigh everything you do. For example, if you had to think about breathing, you wouldn't have time to think about anything else. Or, if you had to think about how to get to and from school every day, you couldn't let your mind wander, listen to music, or enjoy the scenery. What if every time you heard a bird sing, you had to decide which notes you heard or whether to enjoy the song?

At other times, it's best to decide how to handle a situation. When you exercise, you must make a conscious effort to control your breathing. When you're in a new place, you have to think about where you're going and how you're going to get there. If you're studying birds, you want to do more than enjoy the sound of their song.

If you get a flat tire on the way home, your first response may be to kick the car or whimper, "Oh no, oh no, oh no." Pretty soon, however, you'll realize that that response isn't helping you get out of your predicament. Even if you're still upset, you'll force yourself to think calmly. You'll decide to get out the owner's manual and change the tire, call the automobile club for help, or wait for a police officer to arrive.

No matter what problem you're facing, you can choose how to respond. For example, will you get your grocery shopping done faster if you make a list first or if you try to remember what you need when you get to the store? Unless you need only a few items, making a list will probably save time, money, and a return trip to pick up items you forgot. Writing a list is an analytic approach to the task.

On the other hand, if you want to rearrange the furniture in your room, it's probably better to think more spatially and abstractly. You don't want to move any piece of furniture more times than you have to, so it helps to visualize the changes before you start. A person who prefers to think analytically will do this with pieces of paper cut to scale. Someone who prefers to think globally will "see" the room rearranged in his or her mind.

Speed and preference help people decide which way to think. How would you approach shopping for the week? Would you write a list or let the items that you see in the grocery store trigger your memory? There's no wrong or right way to go about shopping or rearranging furniture. You should choose the way that's least frustrating and most satisfying.

MAKE YOUR TASK MAKE SENSE

Motivation—how you can get enjoyment out of the task—also plays a part. Ordinarily, you might have no interest at all in making a scale model of a room. But if you're planning to rearrange furniture, you might suddenly become eager to do just that. The same is true of learning. You may have thought the life cycle of plants was very boring when you studied it in class. But perhaps you've decided to grow herbs in pots on your kitchen windowsill. Now, you really want to know how long it takes seeds to germinate.

Your motivation is very important when you're facing assignments or chores you don't want to do. You can push yourself to take the garbage out or get your taxes done because you know what will happen if you don't. It's bad enough to deal with garbage, but smelly garbage is worse. It's hard enough to do your taxes, but being audited is worse.

When you're doing something unpleasant to avoid future problems, give yourself a reward to work toward. When you have a good reason for doing something, you stop fighting it. Your reward doesn't have to be extravagant, but must be something you'll genuinely love. It could be seeing a movie or taking a nap. It could be soaking in a long, lazy bubble bath. It could be polishing your nails or choosing a new shirt. Choose as a reward one of life's little pleasures. A trip to Italy would be an extravagant reward for taking out the garbage, but if you've accomplished a major goal, that trip may be exactly what you deserve!

THINKING IN TWO PLACES AT ONCE

You'll sometimes hear people speak of being either right-brained (global) or left-brained (analytic). Actually, the very distinction requires left-brained thinking, doesn't it? It assumes that parts are more interesting than wholes. But the idea of being either right- or left-brained is too simplistic.

When people talk of being left-brained and analytic, or right-brained and global, it sounds as if half your brain works harder than the other half. This misconception leads people to see themselves as one type of thinker. If you label yourself in this way, you limit yourself. For example, if you assume that you're left-brained, you may think you're incapable of being creative. Or, if you see yourself as right-brained, you may believe that you're incapable of being logical.

People are always more complicated than labels like these. You may be a fervent sports fan, but that doesn't prevent you from enjoying Mozart's music. You may love to read poetry, but that doesn't make you any less likely to enjoy football. Having a particular talent doesn't mean you can't enjoy, appreciate, or excel in situations that demand other ways of thinking.

Labels are too rigid to define anything as complicated as a human being. What you are is not determined by how others see you. You are always changing and always able to change. No one is locked into one way of thinking or learning. You use your whole brain all the time. You can think analytically or globally, even if you happen to prefer one way.

Think for a moment about how that frees you. Maybe you thought you could never learn to draw or understand math. But that simply isn't true. Anyone can learn how to do anything at all. You just need to change your way of approaching art or math. Once you open yourself up to the possibilities, they become realities.

CHANGING THINKING

Your brain can react to different parts of a task in different ways. For example, people who are musical but untrained in music first will be drawn to music because it moves them. Then, if they learn to read music, they may start to appreciate music in a new way. While their first response to music—"I like this"—may be global, studying music can evoke a more analytical response.

This happens the other way around as well. Think about mathematicians. When they first do computations, they are thinking analytically. But when they reach higher levels of math, they need to bring together—synthesize—information as well as analyze it. If you are programming a computer, you are thinking analytically, but when you use the program to write a letter home, you will begin to think more globally about it. People switch ways of thinking all the time. A painter paints globally, but mixes colors analytically. You may have a dream or a hope, but you have to work toward it step by step.

THINKING STYLES

So you see, your ways of thinking are not as unchangeable as your bone structure or eye color. You can choose your approach to every situation. That means more ways of thinking are open to you than you realized. The trick now is to apply that awareness to your life.

Have you ever quarreled with someone special because you analyze your relationships, and demand a logical reason for everything that happens? You don't have to. You can reach the more intuitive side of yourself. Have you had trouble getting assignments finished on time because you're great at coming up with ideas but slow to get them down on paper? You can change that too.

Before you can change, however, you must know what you can do instead. After you become aware of different ways of doing things, you can apply those strategies whenever the time is right.

CHANGING STYLES

Your tendency to think a certain way may be a matter of style rather than genetic makeup. And you know that hair, clothes, and shoe styles change year in and year out.

Think about the clothes you have in your closet. You have casual clothes to relax in and dressy clothes for special occasions. You have in-between clothes to wear when you're unsure if you're going somewhere casual or formal.

From the clothes you have in your closet, you choose what to wear and when. You let the situation limit your choices. When you're going to a formal dance, you don't even look at your casual clothes. Since you have different kinds of outfits, you don't have to make one outfit serve all purposes.

It's the same with thinking and learning. You have many ways to tackle any given task. This chapter will help you recognize which learning styles you prefer and see how to take advantage of these. It also will show you alternative approaches to getting things done.

Just because you prefer, or tend, to learn one way doesn't mean you can't learn in a different way sometimes. Having a choice is important because there are many ways to do something. Choosing strategies will help you enjoy learning more because you won't find it as frustrating. Think of this as a shopping spree for your mind. You'll be able to choose from a selection of fashions to improve your thinking style.

Wanting to learn

"I can't believe that," said Alice.
"Can't you?" the Queen said, in a pitying tone. "Try again: draw a long breath and shut your eyes."
Alice laughed. "There's no use trying," she said. "One can't believe impossible things."
"I dare say you haven't had much practice," said the Queen. "When I was younger, I always did it for half an hour a day. Why, sometimes I've believed as many as six impossible things before breakfast."
From *Through the Looking Glass* by Lewis Carroll

You perceive information through your senses and intuition. You judge information by reasoning and feeling. To say emotions are linked with reasoning may seem a contradiction, so let's look at how that works.

FEELINGS AND
LEARNING

Many people believe emotions interfere with reasoning. They don't. Actually, emotions help you remember ideas because emotions, such as attraction, affect learning.

What happens when someone catches your eye? You stop and take notice. Then, you begin to find ways to get to know that person better. Attraction is what got you together with your boyfriend or girlfriend. It's also why you learned to play the guitar and why you're reading the latest book by your favorite author. Attraction is a powerful part of learning. It is the first step in understanding someone or something.

Once something has caught your attention, you begin to think about it. As you think, you begin to understand, and understanding helps you remember. Emotions play a big role in learning. Learning begins with the desire to learn. If you like and trust someone, you are more likely to be attracted to that person. Therefore, you will be more likely to learn from that person. On the other hand, if you fear or dislike someone, you will want to avoid him or her. It works the same way with learning itself.

How open you are to learning depends on your willingness or unwillingness to explore. Are you more attentive in art or science, reading or athletics? That probably depends on what you like best. You find it easier to spend time doing something you enjoy. This applies to studying as well. For example, you may find it a tedious chore to memorize the dates of Civil War battles. Yet, you might enjoy memorizing the batting average of every member of your favorite baseball team. You are naturally more willing to devote time and energy to something you enjoy than something you detest. When it comes to learning, your feelings determine your actions.

DO YOU WANT TO DO THIS?

Think about how your emotions are tied to learning. What would you do if someone approached you with a book to read? Asked you to take a personal finance class? Wanted you to write a story? Which would you jump at and which would say "no thanks" to? That's a choice you make whenever you are confronted with an assignment.

It's unrealistic to expect yourself to be thrilled with every single assignment that comes your way. Some you'll immediately be enthusiastic about. Others will be more of a chore than a joy for you. Yet, to do a good job, you have to *want* to do it. There's no magic wand you can wave, so unless you want to learn, you'll be facing an uphill battle. How do you turn boredom into interest? There is a way to get around this problem. Before you tackle any project or subject, find at least one thing to be curious about. Ask at least one question, even if that question is "Why do I have to do this?"

BANISHING BOREDOM

You learn best when the topic interests you. As your interest grows, you pay closer attention and your mind opens to ideas. Not only do you need to be interested when you begin to study, you have to find ways to maintain your interest, or if you lose it, get it back.

Calling on what you already know is one way to make yourself want to learn. Always give yourself something to look for. Ask what is this, why is this the way it is, why did it happen, what caused it to be this way and not some other way, how did this happen, who did this, when did this happen? Give yourself something to discover or uncover and you will have a reason for learning.

You tend to be more interested in something—whether it's weaving or typography—once you know something about it. If a topic means nothing to you, how can you be interested in it? By seeking out information—through people or books, audio- or videotapes, museums or concerts—you can build your interest in a topic. If you're already familiar with a topic, this will help you decide exactly what you want to gain from further study.

GET SOME BACKGROUND

Be sure to review what you already know about a topic or, without realizing it, you'll make your work harder. You'll be starting at square one when you could be way ahead.

Reviewing what you know not only simplifies the learning process but makes you more of a sleuth than a sponge. A sleuth looks carefully at every clue. A sleuth rejects some clues and weighs the importance of others and decides where a piece of the puzzle fits best. A sponge, on the other hand, does not discriminate. It simply absorbs as much as it can and then leaves the rest. A sponge may fill up before it absorbs the really important ideas. To make learning more interesting for yourself, make decisions and draw conclusions about what you are finding out.

If you already know something about a topic, you can look ahead to—anticipate—what you'll be finding out. For example, suppose Elyse is studying the American Revolution in history class. If she recently read a historical novel on Abigail Adams, she'll already have some idea of the events she's studying. Of course, the novel may be historically inaccurate or leave out important details. Yet, because Elyse has read it,

PACE YOURSELF

everything in the text will not be completely new to her.

To gain understanding, you need to distinguish between important ideas and trivial ones. Then, you can focus on the ideas that matter. This is similar to how marathon runners pace themselves during a race. They can't afford to use all their energy in the first couple of miles. They need some reserves to make the final push. Looking ahead, or anticipating, as you read helps you judge when to spend lots of energy on understanding something and when to breeze over it.

When you have a purpose for understanding, you're like a runner who gets a rush of adrenaline near the finish line. The closer you get to finding what you are looking for, the more exciting the race becomes, and you find the energy you need.

KNOWING WHAT'S EXPECTED OF YOU

This sounds daunting doesn't it? Believe it or not, assignments are more overwhelming when you don't know what's expected of you. When you know what you have to do, you're sure about how detailed to get.

What are the chances of an archer hitting a bull's-eye or even the target with a blindfold on? That's what your studies are like if you don't know what's expected of you. If you didn't realize your teacher was expecting a 25-page report and handed in a 2-page report, you'd feel mortified. If you handed in a 25-page report when a 2-page report was expected, you'd be in the same boat.

Knowing what is expected of you gives your work a framework. It helps you decide how to tackle the task and it increases your chances of success immeasurably.

A word of caution here: We don't mean to imply that you should approach your assignments with the sole aim of pleasing your teacher or boss. You need to meet your own expectations also. After all, you're doing the work.

You can make the job more rewarding by having your own set of expectations. They may include taking pride in your work, seeking answers to questions, sticking to the job and staying on track, and keeping your interest in the job. What would you add to the list?

If you have your own expectations, you will be more involved in the project, put more care into it, and feel rewarded by it. If you enjoy the journey, that enthusiasm will shine through on the final product.

Pay attention!

Looking at how your brain works helps you understand your capacity to learn. But other things can improve or diminish your ability to learn. What influence can your emotions, environment, physical surroundings, and frame of mind have on your studies?

You—and your ability to study—are influenced by many things: your mood, the amount of light in your room, hunger and thirst, and much more. The same thing can affect you in different ways at different times. For example, if the sun finally comes out after weeks of spring rain, you may get a burst of energy and tackle your work with renewed enthusiasm. Later in the spring, however, the warm sun and blossoming trees may draw your thoughts away from your work and toward the softball field.

Here we look at some of the things that can affect your concentration: your environment, your emotions, other people, your body, and your personality.

ENVIRONMENT

Your environment includes where you are and what surrounds you. Many small details can make your environment either a good one for studying or a poor one.

For example, sound can affect your concentration a great deal. Some people require complete silence when they study. Others find that silence makes them tense. Do you prefer to study amid absolute silence? Or do you prefer to have some quiet background noise, such as instrumental music? Some people work better when they're surrounded by music; they find it blocks out the sounds of the phone ringing, cars honking, or family members chattering.

The degree of light you need is also a matter of individual taste. Do you prefer bright, soft, or dim light? This is something that may vary with age. Adult students, for example, may find they require brighter light now than they did when they were teen-agers.

What's the best temperature for you? Perhaps you like to work in a cool room, with all the windows open. Your best friend may wonder how you work in that "freezing" atmosphere. But you may find yourself falling asleep the one time you try to study in your friend's warmer room.

How do you like to have the room organized? Do you prefer lots of clutter—notes, open books, souvenirs, class photos, and clipped cartoons all around you? Do you like to have your things neatly arranged, with a place for everything and everything in its place? Or do you think your ideal study room would have nothing in it apart from a desk, a chair, a lamp, and your textbooks?

EMOTION

As you know, your desire to learn depends on many emotional factors. For example, how interested are you in what you have to do? If you are extremely interested, you'll have no problem keeping your mind on your work. But what if you are only mildly interested in what you have to do, or bored out of your skull?

How much do you *want* to do what you *have* to do? If you really want to learn Spanish so that you can visit a pen pal in Mexico, you'll find studying the language easier. But if you think it's a complete waste of your time to learn Spanish, you may spend more energy complaining about the class than working in it.

How persistent can you be when you need to get something done? Can you work toward a goal that's a long way off, such as becoming a doctor, and keep working when the rewards are few and far between? Or do you need to see immediate progress to keep working at something?

How responsible do you feel for getting the task done? Are you relying on yourself? Are others relying on you? Do you feel that others have put too much of a burden on you? Do you do your best when others are counting on you, or do you tend to let things slide?

How much structure do you need when you are working? Do you like to study at a set time and place? Or do you like to vary your study times depending on your mood? Do you find you can study anywhere—on the bus, in the cafeteria, at the beach? Or do you need a peaceful, orderly place?

OTHER PEOPLE

Your interest in working with others depends on the relationship you have with the people you're working with. If you're assigned to work on a report with someone you dislike, your feelings may affect the quality of your work. Ask yourself what kind of work situation would be your ideal.

What work situation do you prefer?

- Do you work well independently?
- Do you work well with one partner?
- Do you work well in small groups?
- Do you work well on a team?
- Do you feel more comfortable with people your own age, older, or younger?
- Do you feel comfortable working with people in authority?

YOUR BODY

Your body affects how well you learn in all kinds of ways. For example, many people find they work best at a particular time of day. Paying attention to your body clock can make your work go smoother and faster. At what time of day do you work best? Are you groggy in the morning but raring to go by evening? Or do you jump out of bed full of energy but collapse by 8 p.m.? Don't try to fight your body clock. Take advantage of it to get things done.

Some people have no problem sitting at a desk for two hours straight. Some sit but have to be moving—drumming their fingernails, swinging their legs back and forth, squeezing a rubber ball. Others have to get up and stretch every 15 minutes or so. Do you learn better when you're sitting at a desk or stretched out on the floor? Or do you like to pace up and down with a book in your hand?

How does hunger or thirst affect you and what do you do about it? Do you find that you can't think of anything else until you get something to eat or drink? Or do you sometimes find yourself ignoring these physical needs and plowing on despite them?

PERSONALITY

How do you prefer to think about things? Do you tend to think analytically or globally? Do you like to get the big picture first and then break it into details? Or do you like to slowly master details and build up to the big picture? Are you usually reflective or impulsive? For example, do you plunge right into a swimming pool, or do you test the water first?

You are affected by different things in different ways at different times. You aren't always hungry or upset, tired or excited. You don't have to be perpetually cheerful and energetic, but you should be aware of what helps or blocks your concentration. To get the most out of studying, you must manage the environmental, emotional, sociological, physical, and psychological stimuli around you.

If you dislike working in groups but have a group assignment, you have to find a way to get comfortable. You could, for example, suggest that every group member complete one part of the assignment independently. You could take on the role of recorder and take notes during the group's meetings. That way, you would be working as part of the group, but also working alone.

On the other hand, you may prefer to work in a group but now face an independent project. Perhaps everyone in your class has to complete a written report on a different topic. How can you make working alone more enjoyable?

First, ask yourself what it is that you like about working in a group. Then, try to make that aspect of group work part of your independent work. Is it the back-and-forth of ideas that you enjoy? Perhaps a friend wouldn't mind listening to your ideas and adding some of her own. Is it the companionship that you enjoy? Perhaps you and a classmate could get together to work on your separate reports. That way, you would be working alone, yet have somebody nearby.

Many times you can change the situation to suit you. Sometimes, of course, you simply have to accept the situation. Whatever the case, you need to make sure you aren't wasting your time. We will explore how you can work comfortably and effectively in any situation.

Distractions

Large or small, pleasing or annoying, anything that takes you physically or mentally away from what you're doing is a distraction. Distractions can have a big effect on how well you do something, no matter what it is. If you become distracted when you're driving, you might miss your exit. If you become distracted when you're watching the Super Bowl, you could miss seeing an exciting touchdown. If you become distracted in class, you could miss the teacher's explanation of an important point completely.

Every day, you have to deal with all sorts of distractions. Some are urgent—your mother has locked her car keys in the trunk and you have to take her an extra set. Some are welcome—a surprise visit from a friend who moved away. Some distractions are little tasks you have to deal with immediately—the dog needs to be walked and you're the only one home; a coworker or classmate calls for some information he or she needs right away.

It is possible to master distractions, however. Have you ever been so involved in reading a book or watching a football game that you failed to hear the doorbell ring or forgot to break for lunch? Your studies don't have to be that consuming. When they aren't the only thing on your mind, however, you need to do something so you can get down to work and stay focused.

Distractions can come from outside of you. Maybe your surroundings are at fault. It might be too hot or too cold, too bright or too dark, too quiet or too noisy, too calm or too busy for you to concentrate. Whatever the cause, you can get rid of such distractions with a little planning. Bring in some more lamps from another room. Put a pillow behind your back. If you can hear neighbors talking, close the window. Or, if you'd rather keep it open, switch on an electric fan to block the voices. If you take the time to make yourself comfortable, you'll be able to focus on your work instead of your discomfort.

You can end or reduce distractions before you begin work on a project or an assignment. One way to do so is to change your environment. This can make it easier for you to study.

MANAGING DISTRACTIONS

To reduce noise and interruptions, you can close your door. By closing your door, you are signaling to others that you don't want to be disturbed. If you find that people knock on your door anyway, put up a "Do Not Disturb" sign. Try letting the answering machine or family members take phone messages for you when you don't want to be disturbed. Even if no one's around to take messages, remember, you don't *have* to answer the phone simply because it's ringing. Ignore it. Otherwise, you may end up engrossed in a friend's dating

HOW CAN YOU GET SOME PRIVACY?

problems instead of your mathematical problems!

It helps to ask others for their cooperation before you act on your plan. Choose a period of time to reserve for work. Then, tell coworkers, family members, or friends that you want to devote those hours to intense concentration. That should mean no interruptions except in an emergency. By consulting others, you're more likely to win their cooperation. This will give you a block of time to concentrate on getting your schoolwork done.

Stick to your schedule as best you can—if you are inconsistent, your support from others will wane. When others see you honoring the time that you set aside for study, they will respect it as well. Be prepared to be firm. Adult students, in particular, may find that family members test their resolve by suddenly demanding their attention as soon as they sit down to work. Try to resist their demands, and any guilty feelings that may stir up. Remember, if you weren't at home, those family members would find someone else to help them.

If you share a room or an office, you might want to coordinate your quiet times. Or, agree on times when the room or office is off-limits to the person you share with. If you work or study at home, it may help if you negotiate a quiet time— several hours in which everyone enjoys quiet activities, such as reading, playing board games, listening to music with headphones, or studying.

Another way to get quiet time at home is to work when others are out. Or, try getting up an hour earlier than anybody else in the family. Remember, others can't know what you need until you ask for it. Give people an opportunity to help by letting them know how. You'll win cooperation more easily if you're nice (but firm) about it. Request instead of demand; ask instead of order.

Make sure your workplace is comfortable. If it's too warm or too dark, you might find yourself fighting off sleep. If it's too bright or too cold, you'll be squinting or shivering instead of working. Sometimes, you can change the temperature simply by adjusting the thermostat. If you can't change the temperature, you can change into shorts or a snuggly sweater.

You can adjust the light by closing or opening shades and turning on or off lamps. You may not be able to buy new lamps or light fixtures, but you can change the light bulbs quite easily. Check the wattage of your light bulbs. Simply getting bulbs with higher or lower wattage may help.

MAKE YOURSELF COMFORTABLE

Usually, you can change your environment relatively easily—you don't need to build skylights or soundproof rooms. If your changes don't work, however, you may need to move to another location. If you've tried changing the light and the temperature, and you've asked others to cooperate but you still lack privacy, you need someplace else to work.

GO AWAY!

Find a place where you won't have to think about answering the phone or worry about what others are doing. If you are at the office, reserve a conference room for yourself. Is there any out-of-the-way nook or cranny in your office or home that you can sneak off to?

If you change locations, you won't have to ignore the phone or worry about visitors. You won't be around to be interrupted. People will find some way to answer their questions and solve their problems without you.

Libraries are designed to encourage studying, so they have a lot to offer. They are quiet, well lighted, and comfortable. Many have public and private workstations. When you're at the library, you won't be interrupted by visitors or distracted by family members laughing at a television show. You'll not only have large tables on which to spread out your papers, but you'll also have many more resources to choose from. In addition to books, you'll be able to use periodicals, microfiche and microfilm, computers and computer programs, audio- and videotapes, and reference rooms.

LIBRARIES ARE HAVENS

And while you're at the library, don't forget that librarians are another source of help. They help you find materials, direct your searches, tell you what services the library provides, and look up information for you. If your particular library doesn't have something you need, the librarians can find out which nearby libraries do. They may be able to get materials for you by borrowing through interlibrary loan systems.

If you are working at the library, you may have to spend a bit of time finding a place that you like. You'll notice that some areas of the library are busier than others, so scout out a place that suits you. Try studying either at the school or public library. Also, many businesses and corporations have private libraries where employees can work in quiet surrounded by lots of references and resources.

NOISE

If you work in an open office, classroom, or study hall, you'll be surrounded by people who can help. But, of course, that can be distracting too. You'll probably have to put up with conversation and noise from others around you. You may find yourself paying more attention to your gossiping neighbors than to your homework.

Some people don't mind background noise. They have a knack of closing out the noise, and that lets them concentrate on what they're doing. If you want to reduce background noise, however, wearing headphones can reduce it. As long as the music doesn't distract you, it may help. If you can get some audiotapes on a subject you're studying, you can kill two birds with one stone.

If you've tried everything to reduce distractions in a common work area but are still struggling, try asking your classmates or coworkers to keep their voices down. If that doesn't work, see if you can move to a seat or office where you will be less likely to be disturbed.

EXPERIMENT

Try any of the suggestions in this chapter at least once. If something works for you, do it. If it doesn't work, try a different approach. Getting rid of distractions will let you get more from your study time. You may need to readjust each time you get down to work.

Make yourself comfortable enough to get things done. Take responsibility for making the time you spend worthwhile. Doing so will pay off in learning and productivity. Your work will show that you put in quality time. The idea is not to achieve perfection, but to achieve balance.

Your workspace should make it easier for you to study. You can make sure it does. You need a place where you can get right down to work, and stay at work during the time you've set aside.

After you've decided where you can work comfortably, decide how you want to design the area and what you want it to contain. Do you like to have lots of things around you when you're working? Or are you a person who requires simplicity? Whatever kind of place you enjoy working in, make sure you have all your supplies on hand. Otherwise, you'll be distracted each time you have to get up to sharpen a pencil or go find a particular book.

A basic requirement for any study or workspace is a writing surface. For many people, that surface will be a desk or table. Others prefer to stretch out on the floor. Of course, even if your concentration is much greater while you're lying on your stomach, you'll probably be able to indulge in that luxury only at home! The most important thing is to be comfortable enough to concentrate, but not comfortable to the point of falling asleep.

MAKE A PLACE FOR YOURSELF

Being aware of how you sit or stand will help you concentrate longer. Support your head, neck, shoulders, and lower back by sitting with good posture. Improper support can lead to tension and fatigue, which in turn can lead to discomfort, backaches, and loss of concentration.

If you feel your muscles tensing, roll your head slowly and stretch your shoulders, arms, and legs to refresh yourself. Taking time to relax or get comfortable will give you greater concentration. The time you take to get comfortable will be time well spent. You want to be able to spend time studying, not thinking about how tired you are or where you're aching. Give yourself a break when you need one.

POSTURE

Your desk or worktable should have enough space for you to spread out your papers, books, and supplies. You might want to keep reference books, such as a dictionary, thesaurus, and atlas, on your desk. Bookshelves and file cabinets can be handy as well.

You may want to add some personal touches, such as plants, posters, a calendar, and a bulletin board. Calendars and bul-

GETTING SET

letin boards can be both functional and decorative. Both are convenient places to write down things you need to remember. Displaying assignments, schedules, favorite sayings, or reminders will help you stay organized, on track, and in control of your work.

The fewer things you leave to memory, the fewer worries you'll have about forgetting something. If you have a lot on your mind, it's likely that you'll forget where things are, who you need to call, what you need to pick up at the store, and so on. Using lists to keep track of things will lessen the clutter in your brain and on your desk.

BE PREPARED

You'll also want to stock up on supplies. Check the following list of supplies to make sure you've got what you need to

Study supplies you may need

- lined paper
- typing paper
- graph paper
- scrap paper
- index cards
- pens
- pencils
- pencil sharpener
- pencil cup
- erasers
- correction fluid
- colored pencils
- colored markers
- highlighter
- ruler
- scissors
- tape
- glue
- folders
- three-ring binder

- notebooks
- file folders
- calculator
- stapler
- staple remover
- hole punch
- rubber bands
- paper clips (different sizes)
- sticky notes
- computer, printer, and printing paper
- disks
- typewriter
- tape recorder
- planning calendar
- encyclopedia
- atlas
- dictionary
- thesaurus

get started. Add to the list if you need additional supplies for a particular project.

Keep your supplies in one place. That way, it'll be easier to pack up if you decide to go to the library or a friend's house to study. If you need to carry some supplies, make sure your pack or briefcase is large enough to hold everything you need.

GETTING
ORGANIZED

After you've set up your workspace, organize your things so that you easily can find whatever you need. Remember, anything can distract you or spur you on, depending on how you handle it. If your workplace is messy and vital material is lost under mounds of papers, your workstation won't work. But if you can find everything easily, you save yourself time, frustration, and last-minute panic.

If you put things away as you finish using them, you'll always know where they are. Once your supplies are set up to your liking, you may even find that you put them away without thinking about it. The less energy you spend on managing your study, the more energy you will have to actually study. Of course, your workspace can be cluttered without necessarily being disorganized. If you can remember that your chemistry notes are at the bottom of the third pile of papers on your bookshelf, fine. If *you* know where everything is, that's all that matters.

Keeping all the papers that come your way on a given day organized is a bit more complicated than organizing your supplies. Every day you have a new batch of papers to deal with. It's hard not to feel like a paper magnet! Making sure that they don't pile up and get lost will require some sort of system. Keep it simple—you want your organization system to be a time-saver, not a full-time job.

Whatever system works for you is the one you should use. Some people prefer to keep things out in piles—no one else knows where anything is. Others prefer to put papers in file folders. They label the folder, insert the papers, and file the folders in a file cabinet.

A third way of storing, organizing, and filing papers is to use a three-ring binder. The three-ring binder acts as a portable file cabinet. Many binders come with dividers and labels to keep your papers organized. You also can buy the dividers separately. To use a binder as an organizer, simply punch holes in the papers and place them where you want them. Add new dividers as you need them. Don't force anything to fit into a category it doesn't belong in. If you can't figure out where to put a piece of paper, ask yourself if you really need it. If the answer is "no," throw it out. If the answer is "yes," make a new category in your binder.

It can help to date papers as you file them. That way, you have a clear record of how classes or projects are progressing. In reviewing your notes chronologically, you can see what topics are becoming more important. Every once in a while, weed out your chronological file. A good time to do this is just before you review for a test, meeting, or presentation. That will save time and energy—you're less likely to review things that aren't important to the test or project.

Also, try to recycle papers instead of throwing them away. Many towns, schools, and offices collect paper for recycling. If yours doesn't, ask why not! You also can reduce waste by using old papers as scratch paper.

A PLAN FOR LEARNING

In Chapter 1, we discussed the importance of making a plan for learning. Now we will give you some strategies for making such a plan.

A plan for learning is based on your strengths, the time and resources you have, and how your work will be evaluated. By working from your strengths, you will use your time productively. You'll also need to work efficiently. You can do so by breaking down assignments into manageable pieces.

ORGANIZING YOUR TIME

Drawing up a schedule will make sure you have the time you need to complete assignments. You'll also find that a schedule makes it easier for you to keep track of assignments. You won't have the time to do something unless you make the time, but knowing what to do with the time is equally important. A schedule is an important tool. As with any other tool, how you use it is more important than having it.

You can use your schedule to decide how much time to devote to any assignment. You can also use it to decide how much time you'll spend on any part of the assignment. If you have a reasonable idea of how much time an assignment will demand, you're less likely to find yourself up at 3 a.m. the day it's due, working frantically to get finished on time.

Assignment schedule
Research/planning–8 hours
- 3 hours at library locating and checking out materials
- 3 hours reviewing materials and taking notes
- 2 hours outlining or making a graphic organizer to follow when I draft my report

Drafting—6 hours
- 1 hour organizing notes
- 5 hours drafting report

Revising—4 hours
- 1 hour evaluating content
- 1 hour reorganizing draft
- 1 hour gathering more information or eliminating information
- 1 hour revising my draft

Editing—2 hours
- Checking grammar, spelling, sentence and paragraph construction

Writing the final report—2 hours
- Typing up report in appropriate format

You've set aside 22 hours for completing the report. If you have four weeks to complete the assignment, you can enjoy a looser schedule. If you have two weeks to complete the assignment, you'll have to make the schedule tighter. If you reduce the number of hours you spend researching, you may not get all the information you need to write a complete and accurate report. However, if you sort your note cards as you go along, you may be able to cut down on the time you spend drafting your report.

Whatever you choose to do, a schedule gives you something to work with and adapt. You may find that you need much more research time than you originally thought, for example, and adjust your schedule accordingly. Always change your plan if it's stopping you from getting the job done. Holding too tightly to a plan that's failing is self-defeating. Give yourself a break whenever you possibly can. Remember, you always have options and you always have choices.

If you break down assignments into manageable pieces, you will be less likely to procrastinate. Procrastination is finding the time to do everything except what you need to do. You're most likely to procrastinate if you put too much focus on the final product. Putting work off and then worrying about it is likely to use much more energy than simply getting down to work.

Instead of having one large looming goal, break down the task so that you can enjoy the satisfaction of reaching many goals. By taking one step at a time, you will reach your goal on time. Each step along the way is as important as the final step. The only way to feel satisfied when you take that last step is to have found satisfaction in the steps that came before.

WHERE DOES TIME GO?

Everyone has the same number of minutes to spend in every day. Despite this, some people get a lot done and some get very little done. Why? Perhaps what matters is not how much time you have but how you spend that time. The issue is quality: "How well do I spend my time?" and not quantity: "How much time do I have?"

To increase the quality of the time you spend, you'll need a schedule. Face the fact that your time is just like money—it's going to get spent, one way or the other. It's up to you to decide what you want it spent on. A schedule is a plan for spending time, just as your budget helps you spend your money wisely and save whenever possible.

Before you make a schedule, try tracking where your time goes. Your day begins when you wake and ends when you fall asleep. But between six and eight hours of each weekday is spent at school or work. During the day, you must attend classes or meetings, and during those periods, you cannot use that time for other things. Instead, you have to plan for these.

Planning for a class or a meeting means that you prepare yourself to get the most out of that time. Reviewing your notes or even reading ahead can help you prepare. By seeing beforehand what you know and what you need help with, you can gain from the class or meeting. Make a list of questions you want answered and check them off as they are discussed.

Working student

Time	Monday	Tuesday	Wednesday	Thursday	Friday	Saturday	Sunday
7am	study	run	study	breakfast meeting	study	work out	
9am	report due	client screening	timesheets due	office	office	library	run
11am	office	↓	office	↓	↓	↓	laundry
1pm	lunch meeting	↓	↓	product demo		↓	study
3pm	office	office	staff meeting	↓		shopping	↓
5pm	↓	↓	↓	↓	↓	housework	↓
7pm	class	study	class	study	class	↓	relax
9pm	↓	relax	↓	relax	↓	relax	↓

High school student

Time	Monday	Tuesday	Wednesday	Thursday	Friday	Saturday	Sunday
7a.m.	swim practice		swim practice	study	swim practice		
9a.m.	↑	↑	↑	↑	↑	↑	church
11a.m.	class	class	class	class	class	swim meet	↑
1p.m.	↓	↓	↓	↓	↓	↓	study
3p.m.	↓	↓	↓	↓	↓	relax	↓
5p.m.	relax	band practice	relax	band practice	relax	↓	tidy room
7p.m.	study	study	music lesson	study	party	babysit	movies
9p.m.	↓	relax	↓	↓	↓	↓	↓

Time	Monday	Tuesday	Wednesday	Thursday	Friday	Saturday	Sunday

Ask about anything on your list that hasn't been covered. Planning for scheduled events is as important as planning for unscheduled events. Your goal is the same—to make the most out of the time you have.

Use the chart on the previous page to see what time you can schedule and what is prescheduled. Fill in the chart so that it reflects your day. Make sure you include any activity you do regularly—from watching TV to exercising.

After you see where your time goes, you can adjust your schedule to include time for studying and completing assignments. Make sure your schedule suits your body clock. Some people are early birds and others are night owls. To decide where you fall on the spectrum, think about when you work most efficiently. Ask yourself the following questions:

At what time of day do I concentrate best? Reserve that time for your most demanding tasks.

At what time of day do I have the least amount of concentration? Reserve that time for relaxing or socializing.

Do I work best in many short study periods or do I need a few long periods of time to work?

Do I work best by myself or with others? If I work best with others, when can I meet with them? If I work best alone, how can I adapt when working on group projects?

As important as it is to have a schedule, it's equally important to adjust your schedule if it's getting in your way. You won't know until you try, so set up a schedule and test it. If it works, keep it. If it doesn't, make a new one.

Take care to avoid overscheduling. Some people tend to take on more than they can reasonably handle. For example, someone may be going to school, working a part-time job, learning to make pottery, volunteering at a local hospital, and trying to keep up with all the latest movies. Face the fact that you don't have the time to do everything you want right now. Decide what activities are vital to you, and which you can leave until another time. For example, you may decide that you enjoy your ballet class so much that you can't give it up. But you may decide that you're not enjoying your swim meets as much as you used to, and give up your place on the swim team. No matter what you decide to give up, make sure it's your decision. Don't give up a hobby you love but keep a part-time job you hate simply because it's "good experience."

When you get an assignment, make a plan for completing each of its steps. Put your plan for completing the assignment in your schedule. Name each step and pick a date for completing it. For small assignments, you may have only one or two steps. For larger assignments, you will have many steps.

Scheduling things in this way will help you manage both your time and your work. If you can't fit in large blocks of study time, set up small study periods several times a day or week instead. Breaking down assignments will also lessen your tendency to procrastinate because you won't see such a huge amount of work looming—you'll see a smaller, more manageable amount.

INTERNAL DISTRACTIONS

Organizing your resources and your time will help you organize your thoughts. But sometimes being prepared to get down to work isn't enough. You have internal distractions as well as external distractions to cope with. Internal distractions can be emotional, such as excitement, nervousness, or depression. They can be physical, such as injuries, exhaustion, or illness. Internal distractions wear many faces, and you have more control over some than others.

These distractions may reflect your physical or mental state. Physical internal distractions that you need to manage include hunger, thirst, fatigue, overexcitement, illness, or injury.

You can avoid hunger or thirst by having a meal or a snack before you begin studying. If you are planning a long study session, fill a tray with healthful snacks, such as fruit, popcorn, vegetables, juice, and water. Having the fuel you need on hand will let you concentrate on what you have to do. If you prefer, you can use your snack time as a break.

If you are overtired or overexcited, you'll find it difficult to think for any length of time. If you don't get enough sleep at night, try taking a nap or resting before sitting down to work. You'll feel refreshed and alert. On the other hand, if you have too much energy, work some off by exercising. Regular exercise and a healthful diet reduce fatigue and keep your energy levels balanced.

SLEEP

Getting too much sleep can dull your alertness almost as much as getting too little sleep. You can make sure you get enough sleep by going to bed at the same time every night, and waking up at the same time every morning. If getting to sleep is a problem, here's a list of tips to help you fall asleep and stay asleep:

Tips for sleeping well

- Avoid caffeine, especially after lunchtime.
- Reduce the amount of sugar, salt, and high-fat foods in your diet, especially at night.
- Get plenty of physical activity—but not too close to bedtime.
- Take time to unwind before bedtime.
- Use your bed only for sleeping and relaxing.
- Keep your bedroom at a comfortable temperature.
- Learn to tune out worries and anxieties at bedtime.
- If you can't fall asleep after 15 minutes, get up and do something else—watch television, read, or do some other relaxing activity. Don't go back to bed until you're sleepy.
- Take a warm bath.
- Focus on repetitive or boring thoughts.
- First tense, then relax each muscle by turn, starting with your toes and moving up to your head.

TIME OFF

If you are ill or have a painful injury, you may have to give yourself some time off. Rest is an important part of healing. Just as driving on a flat tire causes more damage than pulling off the road, you can do yourself more harm than good if you don't take care of yourself when you're unwell.

Putting off work may be better in the long run because you will heal faster. You will be able to work better when you are feeling better. Do only what you feel up to doing. Your attention should be on getting well, not on work. When you're ready to work again, you'll have renewed energy and the ability to concentrate. You can always make up the work you've missed later.

EMOTIONAL DISTRACTIONS

Physical distractions are simpler than emotional ones to deal with because often they're more obvious. For example, if a friend said something mean to you early in the day, it may prey on your mind all day, even though at first you didn't realize that it bothered you. Unresolved arguments or worries can prevent you from concentrating. Nervousness and anxiety also wear you down.

As this chapter discussed earlier, your emotions have a strong effect on your thinking. Sometimes, your emotions will support your efforts to learn. But, as you well know, sometimes emotions or moods can get in the way, too. Think of times in your life when you've been so sad, angry, fearful, or joyful that you couldn't keep your mind on anything except that feeling. Have you ever compounded the problem by adding guilt to the emotional sea that you were swimming in?

When your emotions distract you from work, you may try to distract yourself from your emotions with guilt. But one way of compounding the effect of emotions is to feel guilty about them. If you're feeling guilty, find some way to let yourself off the hook so that you can deal with what's keeping you from concentrating. One way of doing that is to treat yourself as you would treat a friend. Unfortunately, sometimes people treat others more gently than they treat themselves. Stepping back from yourself will give you some perspective on how you're feeling, where those feelings are coming from, and how to cope with them.

The more energy you devote to fighting your feelings, the less energy you'll have to cope with them. So don't fight your feelings, but acknowledge them. Figure out why you're feeling that way. If you're feeling bad about something, figure out some way to make the situation better. If you take care of yourself, you can move on. If you're feeling ready to burst with excitement, share your feelings with others who will be glad for you. Once you have released those emotions, you'll soon be feeling better and ready to return to work.

STRESS

Stress is a distraction that can affect you physically and mentally. Stress can work for or against you when you have a job to do. Life offers all sorts of things to feel stressed about, from responsibilities to relationships. How you see the way you're managing your workload, balancing your time, doing your job, or dealing with others can either increase or decrease your stress level.

You can tell when stress is working for you because you feel pushed to get the work done, but not so much that you are frozen in your tracks. You're interested in what you're doing, and you're finding new and better ways of working. You're learning and studying simultaneously. You're thinking clearly about what you are doing and what you're learning. You're making connections between what you know and what you are discovering. You may find that you're more willing to experiment and ask questions. You're industrious and even innovative in your studying because you're seeking knowledge and understanding.

You'll also be able to tell when stress is working against you. Your mind will jump from thought to thought, you'll worry about things that have happened and what may happen, you'll be so caught up in the would-haves, should-haves, and could-haves that you won't be able to think clearly or for any length of time.

You can feel stressed because too much is demanded of you, or too little. Feeling left out of things can be stressful. You can reduce stress by throwing yourself into work, school, or home. That way, you're not relying on one aspect of your life to satisfy you.

Your body responds to stress physically. Your heart will beat faster, your palms will sweat, you will probably look nervous or tense.

To avoid, prevent, or reduce the toll of stress on your body and mind, you can learn how to change your response to it. For example, if you know that you have several big projects due around the same time, you can lessen the impact by scheduling your time wisely. If something unexpected comes up, you may feel stressed. You can reduce stress using any or all of the following stress-reduction techniques.

Imagery. Imagine that you're resting on a hammock. There's a gentle breeze, the temperature is perfect, your eyes are closed. Does this thought relax you? If so, you've just experienced imagery—an effort to relax by picturing yourself in a peaceful place. Think of something that relaxes you next time you feel stressed.

Deep breathing. If you're stressed, chances are your muscles are tense. Reducing muscle tension may help chase away the stress. Deep breathing is one way to calm your nerves, relax tense muscles, and promote restfulness. It involves inhaling deeply while concentrating just on your breathing. Try to picture the air as it enters and leaves your mouth and nose.

Physical activity. When you feel stress, your body reacts to it by increasing the level of certain chemicals in your blood. These chemicals allow your body to deal with the stress. This reaction is called the "fight or flight" response. Long ago, when our prehistoric ancestors were faced with stress—a hungry lion, for example—these chemicals would give them the energy to either fight the lion or run away from it. Today, we don't face the same kinds of stress. In everyday life, stress is more likely to be psychological—worrying about failing a test or missing a bus, for example—than physical. Our bodies, however, still respond in the same way. Many health experts believe that some major health problems are caused at least in part by stress.

With all this in mind, one way to deal with stress is to engage in some physical activity. Have you ever noticed how good it feels to run around the block, punch a pillow, or do jumping jacks when you're really mad? Exercise gives your body the opportunity to get rid of those stress chemicals.

If you're feeling stressed as a result of personal problems, try to get the support of others. Talk privately with a close friend, a parent, or a guidance counselor. We all need someone to listen. There are people who would like to help you.

Reduce day-to-day stress by allowing yourself enough time to get where you're going. Make commuting easier by finding the easiest route. Relax on your way somewhere by listening to music or books on tape.

Try to ignore rudeness instead of responding with anger. Breathe deeply and slowly to release your tension when it builds up.

Or, try writing about what's bothering you. This can not only help you put things in perspective, but it can help you figure out what to do. If you're feeling disorganized, take the time to get your things in order. Reduce noise but, if you need some background music, choose music that will soothe you.

Look for reasons to feel good. Take time to do things that you enjoy. Find something new and interesting to add to your life: make a new friend, take up a hobby, or try anything that gives you a brighter outlook.

To study or work effectively, you must plan, observe yourself as you work, and evaluate your work and your work habits. Planning can be a tool for getting things done as well as a tool for avoiding obstacles. Good planning doesn't mean perfect planning. If your plan is not working, change it. Plans are supposed to help you get your work done. They are not supposed to get in your way.

PLAN, PLAN, PLAN

A plan is like a blueprint. You build a house from a blueprint, but a blueprint isn't a house. A builder sometimes has to make changes in the blueprint, and you too will have to make changes in your plan for learning. It's easier to change a blueprint than it is to change a house, so be flexible.

Habits are generally pretty wonderful. They keep you from having to think before you do many things that are important—brushing your teeth before bedtime, stopping at a traffic signal, saying "please" and "thank you." Habits are so unconscious that most of the time, you don't even know that you are acting out of habit.

HABITS

Unfortunately, not all habits are good. The problem with habits is that they are so ingrained that they're hard to change. Before you can change any of your habits, you've got to know what they are.

The following inventory of study habits will help you see what you usually do when you study. You can use what you find out about yourself to make the time you spend studying more worthwhile.

WHAT ARE YOUR STUDY HABITS?

So what are your habits of study? To answer that question, mark your response to the following 21 statements as honestly as possible. They are a scale to measure your study habits. As you read the statements, indicate how true each statement is for you by marking, "Never," "Seldom," "Sometimes," "Often," or "Always." Place a check next to each statement in the appropriate space.

Think about how you would study textbooks and other materials assigned to you. Assume that you will be tested on this assignment. Take time to carefully evaluate each statement. After you've filled out the inventory, read on to find out what your score means and what you can do about it.

Estes/Richards Inventory of Study Habits

Name___Tricia Learner_____

When I study,	1 Never	2 Seldom	3 Sometimes	4 Often	5 Always
1. I try to judge how the writer's ideas make sense.			✓		
2. I try hard to remember details, such as names, dates, and technical terminology.		✓			
3. I can't focus on what I read for long periods of time.			✓		
4. I connect what I am reading to ideas learned in other classes.			✓		
5. I take time to copy my notes before I study them.				✓	
6. I find it hard to keep my mind on my work.				✓	
7. I try to understand what I read so that I could say it in my own words.			✓		
8. I reread materials that I already understand.			✓		
9. I tend to daydream.				✓	
10. I think of ways to apply what I learn.			✓		

When I study,	1 Never	2 Seldom	3 Sometimes	4 Often	5 Always
11. I go over what I read page by page in order to remember the details.					✓
12. I need time to get "warmed up" to the task.					✓
13. I relate what I read to real-life experience.			✓		
14. I take extensive notes on what I'm reading.				✓	
15. I am likely to waste time getting started.			✓		
16. I find what I read for class meaningful to me.		✓			
17. I underline or set off in some way large parts of what I read.					✓
18. I find my study periods are interrupted by noise, visitors, or telephone calls.				✓	
19. I find assigned reading to be interesting.			✓		
20. I try to memorize word for word most of the information I have been assigned to read.			✓		
21. I have to be in the right mood before I start to work.				✓	

Estes/Richards Inventory of Study Habits scoresheet

Instructions:

1. Write the score for each item response on the line next to the item number.

2. Add the numbers in each column.

3. Write the total score for each column at the bottom of that column.

I	C	D
1. _3_		
4. _3_	2. _2_	
7. _3_	5. _4_	3. _3_
10. _3_	8. _3_	6. _4_
13. _3_	11. _5_	9. _4_
16. _2_	14. _4_	12. _5_
19. _3_	17. _5_	15. _3_
	20. _3_	18. _4_
		21. _4_
I = 20	C = 26	D = 27

Initiative
score = _20_
Total of 1, 4, 7, 10, 13, 16, and 19.

Compulsivity
score = _26_
Total of 2, 5, 8, 11, 14, 17, and 20.

Distractibility
score = _27_
Total of 3, 6, 9, 12, 15, 18, and 21.

Estes/Richards Inventory of Study Habits

Name_____

When I study,	1 Never	2 Seldom	3 Sometimes	4 Often	5 Always
1. I try to judge how the writer's ideas make sense.					
2. I try hard to remember details, such as names, dates, and technical terminology.					
3. I can't focus on what I read for long periods of time.					
4. I connect what I am reading to ideas learned in other classes.					
5. I take time to copy my notes before I study them.					
6. I find it hard to keep my mind on my work.					
7. I try to understand what I read so that I could say it in my own words.					
8. I reread materials that I already understand.					
9. I tend to daydream.					
10. I think of ways to apply what I learn.					

When I study,	1 Never	2 Seldom	3 Sometimes	4 Often	5 Always
11. I go over what I read page by page in order to remember the details.					
12. I need time to get "warmed up" to the task.					
13. I relate what I read to real-life experience.					
14. I take extensive notes on what I'm reading.					
15. I am likely to waste time getting started.					
16. I find what I read for class meaningful to me.					
17. I underline or set off in some way large parts of what I read.					
18. I find my study periods are interrupted by noise, visitors, or telephone calls.					
19. I find assigned reading to be interesting.					
20. I try to memorize word for word most of the information I have been assigned to read.					
21. I have to be in the right mood before I start to work.					

Estes/Richards Inventory of Study Habits scoresheet

Instructions:

1. Write the score for each item response on the line next to the item number.

2. Add the numbers in each column.

3. Write the total score for each column at the bottom of that column.

I	C	D
1. _____		
4. _____	2. _____	
		3. _____
7. _____	5. _____	
		6. _____
10. _____	8. _____	
		9. _____
13. _____	11. _____	
		12. _____
16. _____	14. _____	
		15. _____
19. _____	17. _____	
		18. _____
	20. _____	
		21. _____
I =	C =	D =

Initiative	**Compulsivity**	**Distractibility**
score =_____	**score =_____**	**score =_____**
Total of 1, 4, 7, 10, 13, 16, and 19.	Total of 2, 5, 8, 11, 14, 17, and 20.	Total of 3, 6, 9, 12, 15, 18, and 21.

FINDING YOUR
SCORE

This inventory will yield three scores—one for initiative, one for compulsivity, and one for distractibility. (We'll explain those words once you have your score figured. Don't worry about your scores right now—sometimes a high score is good, sometimes not.) Follow these steps to get your three scores:

1. Look again at the answer columns on the scale where you checked "Never," "Seldom," "Sometimes," "Often," and "Always." The columns are numbered 1, 2, 3, 4, and 5. All answers of "Never" are worth one point, all answers of "Seldom" two points, all answers of "Sometimes" three points, all answers of "Often" four points, and all answers of "Always" five points. Write down the value of each answer you've given.

2. Now, transfer these numbers to the scoresheet. Write the value of your response to item 1 in the blank next to the number 1 on the scoresheet. For instance, if you checked "Sometimes" for item 1, write 3 on the scoresheet next to number 1. To see exactly how this is done, look at the sample scale and scoresheet.

3. To figure your initiative score, add the values of your responses to items 1, 4, 7, 10, 13, 16, and 19. These are the responses you have written in the first column of the scoresheet.

4. To find your compulsivity score, add the value of your responses to items 2, 5, 8, 11, 14, 17, and 20. These are the responses you have written in the second column of the scoresheet.

5. For your distractibility score, add the value of your responses to items 3, 6, 9, 12, 15, 18, and 21. These are the responses you have written in the third column of the scoresheet.

YOUR INITIATIVE
SCORE'S MEANING

What does your score on initiative mean? A high score (above 25) is good. Think about the meaning of *initiative. The World Book Dictionary* defines *initiative* as: "The active part in taking the first steps in any undertaking; readiness and ability to be the one to start something; enterprise."

Initiative is really more than a simple habit of study.

Initiative is tied to the habit of starting and finishing a job because you care about it. The root meaning of the word *initiative* is "to begin," as you can see in related words like *initiate* and *initial*. So, initiative refers to the kind of start you make when you study.

Initiative also includes follow-through. In any activity, how you start has everything to do with how you follow through. For example, how you stand to receive a pitch in baseball has everything to do with how you begin your swing, which has everything to do with how the bat makes contact with the ball. The same relationship between beginning and follow-through holds for almost everything, from the simple act of walking to the complex skill of driving a car. It holds just as strongly for what you do to perform your best in school.

The initiative scale describes habits you will easily recognize if you are a motivated student, such as trying to make sense of what you study, connecting new ideas to ones you already know, and putting things in your own words. What do these habits have in common? They all imply that you are on top of your work and care about what you are doing.

If your initiative score is low (below 14), look carefully at the items that make up the scale and decide which you could change to help you study better. Make a conscious effort, for example, to connect new ideas to your own life. If you do, you may find that what you are studying is more interesting, easier to follow, and easier to remember.

You can do many things to take initiative when you study, especially when your study involves reading, as so much study does. The following suggestions are like a menu of your options. You can opt for some or all of them.

INCREASING YOUR INITIATIVE

Before you begin reading, you can:
1. Think about the title of the selection, asking yourself what you already know about the topic.
2. Read any questions or summaries at the end of the sections or chapters, to see what the writer thought were the main points.
3. Notice whether the chapter is divided into sections. The divisions usually will be marked with italics or boldface. If so, this will help you take in the chapter bite by bite

instead of swallowing it whole. Bite off only as much as you can chew.

4. Turn subheadings into questions that you can answer as you read. Someone once said that comprehension is having your questions answered. If that's so, comprehension depends on curiosity—the better your questions, the better the answers may be.

5. Examine all pictures and graphs so they will be easy to refer to when the text mentions them.

6. Make a few preliminary notes about what you expect to learn from the reading. If possible, compare your notes with those of classmates or friends who are doing the same assignment.

As you read, you can:

1. From time to time, stop to put what you read into your own words. Say to yourself what you understand as you understand it.

2. Frequently stop to ask yourself whether your studying is going well and whether you really understand what you're studying. If you're having a problem, figure out what's causing it. Is it a word you don't understand? Look it up or ask someone. Is it an idea you don't get? Look in the index of the book or check another source to find a simpler explanation. Above all, don't ignore your confusion—take the initiative and do something to clear it up.

3. Try to link the ideas you are reading to ideas you've already learned. Make a conscious effort to judge how the ideas you are studying make sense. Try to think of everyday examples that illustrate the principle you're trying to learn.

4. If possible, underline or make notes as you read. Here's another chance to put the information into your own words. Think of yourself as an active seeker of knowledge, not a passive vessel waiting to be filled.

After you read, you can:

1. Close your book and try to remember the passage you have just read.

2. Think back to the questions you started with. Try to

answer them without looking at the book.
3. Make a note of anything you can't remember so you can ask your teacher for more explanation or information.
4. Ask yourself how your understanding has changed. Examine how much you've learned.

What does your score on compulsivity mean? On this scale, a high score is not necessarily good. Compulsive habits are things that people overdo. It's a good idea, for example, to wash your hands frequently. But hand-washing goes beyond a good habit if you wash your hands 20 or 30 times a day, or if you have to wash your hands every time you shake hands with another person.

YOUR COMPULSIVITY SCORE'S MEANING

A high compulsivity score (above 25) suggests you may be doing *more* work than you need to. You actually may be wasting some study time by overworking. Ask yourself seriously about your study habits. Do you try to memorize every single word of your text or copy your notes before you use them? Look at each compulsivity item you've checked on the inventory and ask yourself, "Is it really necessary for me to do this?"

Remember this: Success in studying depends partly on doing the job right, but even more on doing the right job. If you're spending hours every night doing work that doesn't need to be done, then your effort will be completely wasted.

You can do lots of things to strike a balance between too much work and too little. It's important to make sure you do the right job and do it right. Here are some options to consider that might make your work habits most effective and efficient.

1. Think about your study goals. What are you studying for? For example, are you reading for a class discussion? If so, think of the questions that the discussion can answer. Are you reading for a test? What kind of test? If it's an essay test, you can study for main ideas to which you add details. If it's a multiple-choice test, look for details that are likely to be included. If you're clear about why you're studying, you can focus your energy on reaching that goal.

2. Decide your priorities. Put each task—reading, writing, preparing a report—into a specific order and schedule. When you have some perspective on each task, you'll see just how much time and effort you need to devote to it. A good approach may be to layer priorities—for each study session, each week, and each semester.

3. Think about the kinds of questions you usually see on tests in the class for which you are studying. If you were making the test for this material, what would you include? In other words, what would you ask of people to find out if they understood what you've been assigned to study? The answers to such questions will help you get more out of studying for tests.

4. If you have been given questions to use in completing an assignment, be sure you understand their meaning and scope before you begin studying. Ask for clarification if you have a shadow of doubt about what you're really being asked to do. Clarifying questions in this way will help you separate main points from details.

5. Try to imagine where you will have to recall what you've learned. Will you have to report back to a small group? Make a report to the entire class? Participate in a debate? Take a quiz? Adapt your studying to the way you'll be using what you learn.

What does your score on distractibility mean? A high score (more than 25) suggests that you do not concentrate closely when you study. Distractions are a part of life for everyone. But to get things done, you sometimes need to sidestep them. Perhaps you need to master some strategies for coping with those distractions.

Remember, the two kinds of distractions are external distractions, such as noise and other people, and internal distractions, such as worry or fatigue. In general, try to reduce external distractions and cope with internal distractions, at least until they can be put right.

Reread the tips on dealing with external distractions. You may find it helpful to set interim goals, such as saying, "For the next 10 minutes, no matter what happens, I will not stop reading." As soon as you've mastered concentrating for 10 minutes, move the time up to 12 minutes and then to 15. Keep expanding your concentration until you can keep your mind on your work for any length of time.

Internal distractions may be more difficult to control. But some simple things will help here, too. For example, if you can't concentrate because you keep thinking about all the other things you're not getting done, make notes of things you'll do later—feed the dog, call a friend, take out the garbage. (Some things will just have to wait!)

If something is upsetting you to the point of interfering with your work, ask yourself what you can do about the situation. Perhaps a friend has a habit of making jokes at your expense. You'd probably rather not make a scene, but if the jokes are hurting your feelings, confront your friend. Be honest. Don't accuse your friend of being a jerk; simply describe how the jokes make you feel. You'll find that simply talking about the problem will release some of the tension you've been carrying around inside.

What if it's somebody in authority who's doing something that bothers you? For example, perhaps your teacher has a habit that drives you crazy, such as mispronouncing words. Obviously, you can't ask the teacher to change that habit to suit you. But you can try to make the habit less irritating. Try making a game out of the situation. Tell yourself, "If she does it 5 times this week, I'll buy myself a magazine. If she does it 10 times, I'll get an ice cream cone."

If fear of a test has you in a dither, make up a funny story about the worst thing that could happen if you don't do well. If worry has you down, take a minute to breathe easier. Remember, 90 per cent of what people worry about will either never happen or is outside their control. Why waste energy on it? If you're worried about not understanding what you're studying, do something to increase your understanding at least a little. Rome wasn't built in a day, it is said, and neither will your knowledge. Take it easy, bit by bit, all in good time.

CONTROLLING
DISTRACTIBILITY

If these ideas work for you, make the best of them.

1. Put yourself in a proper mood for study. Try to psych yourself up for spending a certain amount of time studying. Challenge yourself. Everyone tries to avoid work at one time or another, but for those who get the job done, it is usually "mind over matter." In other words, set your mind to the fact that a particular task must be done.

2. Approach each study task believing you'll succeed. It is critically important to approach each step expecting to get the job done and done well.

3. Develop a study system that works for you. Just as there are lots of ice cream flavors and what one person likes may not appeal to another, study systems are a matter of individual preference. Figure out what works for you.

4. Be active in your study. Take notes as you read. Rehearse what you understand. (It's perfectly all right to talk things over with yourself when you're studying!)

5. If possible, divide the load with someone else. Form a study group with one or more people. Say, for example, you check out one source of information and your study partner checks out another. When you get together, you can discuss it and get the benefit of two thoughts on the same topic. Share your reactions and understanding. Test each other.

From time to time, go through the study habits items again and watch your answers change. Answer items on the scale as you think about a course you're acing. Then do the scale again as you think about a course you're struggling in. Look at how your answers differ for the two courses. See whether some of the things you do in the first course might help in the second.

USING THE STUDY HABITS INVENTORY

Remember to consider *what* you are doing as well as *how* you are doing it. Whenever you finish a project, don't rush on immediately to the next assignment. Think about what you did that made this assignment easy or difficult. Be sure to use what works for you the next time. As soon as you start to struggle, think of other ways to do something. That way, you can build up a store of strategies that work.

Looking back at what you've done is also a way of getting rid of some habits that prevent you from accomplishing something. If you were trying to eat something that was too hot, you'd wait for it to cool off. When it comes to studying, however, you may forget to do the obvious. This happens when you forget to focus on whether you're making studying easier or harder for yourself.

You have so many different ways to approach a single

assignment. Like an athlete preparing for a game, you have to train, then play, look at how you played, then change your technique. By doing this, an athlete is always sharpening his or her skills. You can do the same. You may not have postgame tapes to watch, but you can look at what you've done and decide what to keep or change next time.

Ask yourself these questions before you begin to work on the assignment:

How much time do I have to do this?

What steps do I need to take to do this?

How long will I need to finish each step?

Do I have enough time, or will I have to adjust my step-by-step plan?

How will I make myself want to do this?

Can anybody help me or do I need to do this myself?

Is there anything in the way of getting the job done?

How can I lessen distractions?

As you work, ask yourself the following:

What will I do to stay or become interested in this?

Is my plan working, or do I need to adjust it in any way?

What can I do differently?

After you finish, ask yourself these questions:

What would I do again next time?

What would I do differently?

Did I stop when things weren't working and change my plan?

If you do this every time you work on an important assignment, you'll learn a lot about your approach to studying. You'll start to see what works for you and what doesn't. Often, students get so caught up in what they have to do that they don't give themselves a chance to do it well. The better you understand your study habits, however, the greater your chance of success.

A lot of the information in this chapter may be completely new to you. Chances are you've never given a thought to how you learn, whether you should change your study habits, where you work most comfortably, or what you can do about distractions. It may seem a lot to think about. It is.

Be content to simply think about these things for a while. Don't try to change your study methods, rearrange your study place, form a study group, and reorganize all your papers immediately. If you try to make a lot of big changes at the same time, you'll end up feeling tired and discouraged.

First, spend some time thinking about what you'd like to change. Ask yourself what you could change easily, and what would take more effort. It might help to write a list of changes you'd like to make.

Then, pick a small change that you can make easily. Suppose, for example, you decide to start keeping your notes in file folders instead of piling them up in a corner of your room. Wait until you're used to storing your notes this way before you make another change.

By making small, gradual changes—all the while asking yourself what's working and what's not—you'll gradually take control of your studying. Studying won't seem such a daunting, mysterious ritual. Instead, studying will become something that you know how to do, and do well!

"It all depends on how we look at things, and not how they are in themselves."

C. G. Jung

3

LEARNING STRATEGIES

✎ Staying focused   ✎ Managing information

✎ Keeping on track   ✎ Your learning strategies

✎ Reading   ✎ Graphic organizers

✎ Taking notes   ✎ Reports and projects

You have innumerable ways of thinking and learning. Take a moment to think about the ways you enjoy most and that work best for you. Would you prefer to learn about a country by reading a book, watching a movie, listening to tapes, building models of typical homes, doing an experiment, solving a problem, role-playing, talking to others, going to a museum, or by cooking and eating foods of that country?

Any of these activities are good ways to learn. Doing one thing wouldn't prevent you from doing another. In fact, each activity would prepare you to learn more. For example, if you were taking a course in the history of ancient Greece, you could learn more from the course by doing something that would prime you for thinking about Greece. You might read Greek mythology, look at pictures of Greek temples, make a map, go to a Greek restaurant, or simply list everything that comes to mind when you think of Greece.

Staying focused

If you give yourself some background knowledge on any subject before you begin to study it, you will find yourself reading to answer your own questions. Having some questions about Greece will help you read about it critically. You'll be able to tell which details are important to understand and which are not. To get the most out of any article or textbook, you must read it actively. Jot down or highlight important information. Keep a list of questions you want answered as you read. Do anything that keeps your mind focused on and curious about the subject.

After you finish reading, mentally summarize what you've just read. If you still have questions, find the answers. Studying begins before you open a book and continues after you close it. That's because you are the most important part of your studies.

Review the study habits inventory. What do your answers tell you about yourself? Make your own learning profile—you can write it, draw it, or diagram it. As long as it's an accurate self-portrait, it will help you pick learning strategies to suit your strengths. Try making two profiles, one of where you are now and one of where you'd like to be. Do this in any way you find most interesting and helpful.

You study a topic to learn about it. But, as you may know from personal experience, studying doesn't always lead to learning. To learn, you have to know what you're looking for. If you don't have a reason to study, you will be searching in the dark. If you don't know what you're looking for, how will you know when you find it?

Studying is simply gaining control over the ways you understand. You gain that control by knowing what strategies to use when you study, how to use the strategies, and when to use a particular strategy. By knowing the strategies you have, you are giving yourself options. By knowing how to use the strategies, you can pinpoint which will work best for you. By knowing when to use the strategies, you can choose the best tool for the job.

You wouldn't build a house using only a hammer. You'd need a variety of tools in your toolbox to help you do many jobs. But it takes more than having a tool to do the job—unless you know how to use a particular tool, it won't work. True, you could probably trim a board by hammering it. But how hard and how long would you have to labor? And, if you finally did break off the end with a hammer, would the board be of any use? You know a saw is better for cutting a board down to size. Both hammers and saws are useful tools but they're suited to different tasks. Study strategies are tools for learning, but you must know how and when to use them. You'll throw yourself into learning with more confidence when you have a good set of tools to finish the job—and when you know which tool to pick.

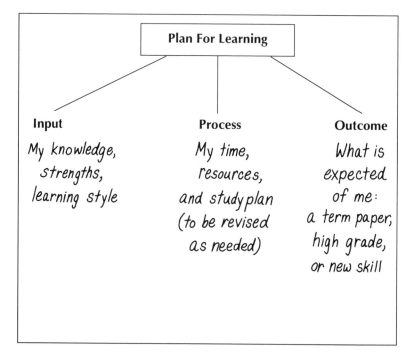

Managing information

When something makes sense to you, your brain can link it to other facts, ideas, memories, or images. Your brain always looks for patterns because it sorts and stores information in groups or chunks. When your brain doesn't know what to do with a piece of information, it tells you that you don't understand. Your brain needs you to make things clear so that it can sort, store, remember, and recall the information.

It's easier to remember small bits of information than large blocks. Think of it in terms of gathering rocks to build a house. At first, you might think that if you use only boulders, your house will be built faster. But try picking up a boulder! If you choose rocks that you can manage, you'll be able to build your house. Here are some ways to break down information so that it's the right size for you to understand it.

You can sort information in many ways. By looking for similarities or differences, you can put information into categories that will help you understand. You can sort information by characteristics, such as size, shape, color; states of being, such as alive or dead, animate or inanimate, real or make-believe; time, such as past, present, or future; or subject, such as history, geography, science, math, and literature.

CLASSIFY

You can make your classifications more useful by grouping chunks of information to expand on the examples of each listing.

CHUNK OR GROUP

For example, suppose you are sorting information about the prairie style of architecture. Under that heading, you can group each architect with a famous building designed by him or her—and any other supporting details that will help you understand. For example, you could write, "Frank Lloyd Wright believed that buildings should 'grow' from their sites. He believed the building that best accomplished this on the Midwestern prairies was a low, horizontal home."

You can understand anything more easily by finding the underlying patterns or principles that hold it together. For example, to fully understand the prairie style of architecture, it would help to know what influenced the designs of Frank Lloyd Wright.

PATTERNS OR PRINCIPLES

By looking at the big picture, you can see the details that make up the whole and how they fit together.

FIND THE CONTEXT

To see how Frank Lloyd Wright accomplished his goal of building homes that "grow" out of the landscape, try looking at several examples of his work. If you live in an area where he built homes, visit some of the homes so you can experience the effect of his designs yourself. If that's impossible, look at photos or drawings to see what his homes are like. Notice what design elements are repeated from house to house. Browse through a biography of Wright. This will help put his work in context for you.

SUMMARIZE

Summarizing is a concise way of stating what you've learned. By summarizing, you express what you've learned in a sentence or two. For example, "By using wood and earth-toned building materials, Frank Lloyd Wright made his homes fit naturally into the environment. You get the feeling that his homes sprang up from the earth because their low, horizontal layout spreads across the land like the prairie itself."

Keeping on track

Learning is a gradual process, made up of many steps. As you move through the process, you have to know if what you're doing is working. If it isn't, you have to know what to change. You have to be flexible, willing to change your course at any time along the way.

Many of the things you do to keep on track, you may do without realizing it. Have you ever found your mind wandering as your eyes continue to read? Without thinking, you probably go back to where you last remember attending to the text. If going back and reading with attention puts you back on track, you can continue reading—until you get to a passage that confuses you. When you realize that you no longer understand, stop reading and ask yourself these questions:

What do I already know that might help me understand this?

What exactly don't I understand?

Where can I find the information I need to be able to clear up my confusion?

If you do this when you don't understand, you'll avoid a lot of frustration and feel less likely to give up on the task and yourself. You can't always grasp everything immediately. Everyone, no matter how smart or studious, has to work to understand something sometime. So don't put extra pressure on yourself or kick yourself for not becoming an instant expert. The goal is not to understand everything right away. The goal is to help yourself understand.

WATCH FOR CONFUSION

You need to be aware of your thinking as you read a book, listen to a lecture, or follow directions. By staying alert to whether you understand the information, you can act as soon as you get confused. If you know you don't understand what you're reading, you can go back in the text and reread. Or, you can skim ahead to see if things get clear. Once you find what you're looking for, go back and continue reading. If you don't understand what a lecturer is saying, you can ask him or her to explain. You have to make sense of directions before you can follow them. This kind of monitoring will help you stay on the right path. If you plow ahead without understanding, you will block your chance to learn.

LOOK AHEAD

You can open yourself up to learning even before you crack open a book, attend a class or a lecture, or try to solve a problem. Looking ahead, or anticipating what you'll learn, is the first step you need to take. If you call up what you know, believe, and feel about a topic, you set the stage for further learning. You're piquing your curiosity and giving yourself a reason to learn.

You can begin by asking yourself the following questions:

What is this article (book, chapter, lecture, or demonstration) going to be about?

What do I know about this subject?

What do I want to learn about this subject?

Why do I want to learn about this?

What do I expect to find out?

Questioning yourself like this will make it easier for you to absorb information. Approaching your studies with an open mind will help you make sense of what you learn. You may find yourself adding to what you already know, confirming what you already know, replacing out-dated or incorrect information, or disagreeing with what you find out. Any of those reactions are possible. But unless you look ahead first, you will be less involved in your own learning.

If you're unfamiliar with a topic, it may be difficult to figure out what you already know about it. You may find it helpful to work with another person or a small group of people. By working with others, you can share information and help one another fill in the blanks.

These activities are like warm-up exercises for your mind. Just as stretching prepares your muscles, heart, and lungs for a workout, these activities open your mind to the demands of study. In giving yourself reasons to learn, you become an active questioner and seeker of information. When you approach your studies with a purpose, your mind is better prepared to absorb, sort, store, and remember all the information you come across.

Details

> Jazz has its roots in the folk songs and dance music of African Americans in the 1800's.

> Fully developed jazz probably started in New Orleans in the early 1900's.

> Blues, which contributed to the development of jazz, also began in the United States.

Main idea

The type of music known as jazz has been called the only art form that originated in the United States.

Your learning strategies

Remember the steps to learning on page 22? First, you need to know what strategies you can choose from. Then, you should know how to use a particular strategy. Finally, you must know when to use that strategy. We describe different study strategies on the following pages. These strategies set the stage for learning—they are the "what" in the process. The explanation provides the "how," and before you read or listen to a lecture is the "when."

Try out several of these activities to decide which ones work best for you. You may want to keep this book out when you study to remind you of what you can do, how to do it, and when to do it.

BRAINSTORMING

Write down everything you can think of about a topic. Don't censor yourself at all. Don't judge the ideas, just record them. Allow yourself enough time to warm up and get going. You'll notice that writing down one idea will trigger others.

After you have your list, you may want to classify or organize your ideas in some way. Graphic organizers are helpful tools for linking ideas. You'll find that you can use them before you read, as you read, and after you read. As you become more knowledgeable on a topic, change your graphic organizers to reflect that new learning. We'll look at graphic organizers in detail later in this chapter.

PReP stands for the pre-reading plan, a strategy developed by Judith A. Langer. This study method can help you get more out of assigned reading. Try following these steps before you read assigned material.

PRₑP

Step 1 What do you think of?
Name anything that comes to mind when you think of the topic. Do the exercise with the examples to see how this study technique works.

Example:
What do you think of when you hear the name Picasso?
art
Spain
paintings
sculptures
The Art Institute of Chicago
Gertrude Stein
The Spanish Civil War

Step 2 Why do you think that?
Explain why you made connections between the topic and the things that came to mind.

Art—I think of art because I know that Picasso was an artist.
Spain—I think of Spain because I think that's where he was born or lived.
Paintings—I think of paintings because I know he painted.
Sculptures—I think of sculptures because I think I saw some in the Sculpture Gardens at the National Gallery of Art in Washington, D.C.
The Art Institute of Chicago—I think of the Art Institute because that's where I first saw Picasso's work.
Gertrude Stein—I think she wrote about him.
The Spanish Civil War—I think some of his work was a protest against the war.

It helps to group information now. How might you group these ideas with the ones you came up with?

Step 3 Rework your original ideas.
This step is helpful if you are working with others because you can adapt your original ideas as you learn from them.

> I realize that Picasso is a famous and important artist because his work is in museums and he's created different types of artwork.

REQUEST

You need a partner to do ReQuest effectively. ReQuest, developed by Anthony Manzo, stands for *Reciprocal Question*ing. You and your partner take turns asking and answering questions. You can also use ReQuest when studying in groups.

1. Each of you reads the first sentence or paragraph of a text.
2. The person who is asking questions keeps the book open. The person who is answering questions closes the book.
3. The questioner asks any question about what you have finished reading.
4. The answerer answers the question as best he or she can. Then, he or she comments on the quality of the question.
5. Continue the process until everyone feels confident asking questions. The last question to be asked before reading independently should be, "What do you think we are going to find out?"

By asking questions, you will tap into what you already know on the topic and become curious to find out more.

CUBING

Cubing, developed by E. and G. Cowan, gives you a chance to write down what you know. Writing gives you time to pull your thoughts together. It also records your original response to a topic. In addition, it lets you make free associations instead of censoring yourself.

You may use a square box for your cube. Measure one side so you know how large to make the pieces of paper you'll use as cube coverings.

1. Make up your cubing questions and write them on each cube covering. Tape a cube covering to each side.
2. Set a time limit of two to five minutes for answering all the questions.
3. If you are doing this with a partner or in a group, share your responses so that you can all learn from one another.

Make up your own cubing questions.

K-W-L prepares you to learn by helping you tap into your present knowledge, identify what you need to find out, and sort through the information you've learned. *K* stands for what you *Know*; *W* stands for what you *Want* to learn; and *L* stands for what you've *Learned*.

K-W-L

The K-W-L process, developed by Donna Ogle, allows you to zero in on your study topic and use your time most effectively. Each step keeps you focused on your study goals.

1. Using the diagram below as your guide, write in the first column everything you know about your study subject. Now group this information into categories.
2. In the second column, write down what you would like to find out as you read. Use your information categories in the first column to help you decide where you'd like to learn more.
3. Read the text.
4. In the third column, write down what you've learned. Place the information in the categories you listed in the first column. Add new categories or rename your categories as you see fit.

What do I know?	What do I want to learn?	What did I learn?
Spiders - have 8 legs - lay eggs - build webs - eat insects and other animals	What spider webs are made of. Why spiders don't get caught in their own webs.	Spider webs are made of silk. Spider silk is the strongest natural fiber known. Not all strands in a spider web are sticky. Spiders know which ones are not sticky and walk only on those.

Categories

a. *body/physical traits*	e. *scientific classification*
b. *behavior*	f.
c. *reproduction*	g.
d. *diet*	h.

Clustering, developed by Gabriele Rico, is a tool for helping you unlock ideas whenever you want to express yourself—whether in a report, a speech, a short story, or a poem.

1. Write down a key word in your topic.
2. Through brainstorming, come up with other words and ideas linked to what you've written.
3. Circle each word and draw a line to any other word you linked to it.

Here is a sample cluster for study. Add your own ideas to the cluster.

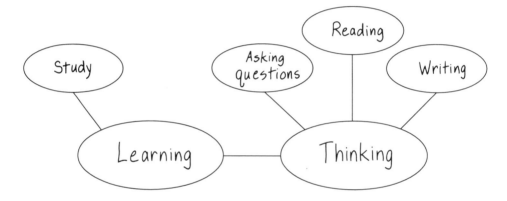

Reading

No doubt, studying involves reading. But your approach differs when you're reading to study rather than to pass the time. When you study, you read to remember information, perhaps names, dates, or events. This is different from reading for pleasure because your mind is involved with the text in a completely different way.

Whenever you read, you judge or evaluate the content. Try to answer these questions: Do you find yourself considering the source? Are you willing to change your mind about what you thought was true? Do you search for confirmation of your conclusions as you read?

You're thinking about what you're reading, not how to read it. But if you examine what you're doing, you'll realize that you're reacting to what you read. You may like what you read because you agree with what the author is saying. You may dislike it if you disagree. You may change your mind about something because of what you read. Reading involves YOU.

Your reaction to what you read depends largely on how much you already know about a topic. For example, you know that the sun rises in the east and sets in the west. If a book says otherwise, you will not accept what the author is saying. On the other hand, if the author is discussing family life in medieval Spain, you may be in no position to challenge a statement. You have to read what other authors say on the topic.

To get the most out of what you read, actively search for new ideas and reshape your thoughts as you find them. You'll welcome and adopt some of the ideas you come across, while rejecting others.

Applying what you know about a topic to what you read will help you predict information to come. You'll base your learning on the nature of what you read, whether it's a poem, an article, a story, a how-to book, a map, a diagram, a graph, or a table. You'll make sure you are understanding by asking yourself questions as you read. You'll check to make sure you understand and look for explanations when you don't.

PREDICT WHAT'S COMING

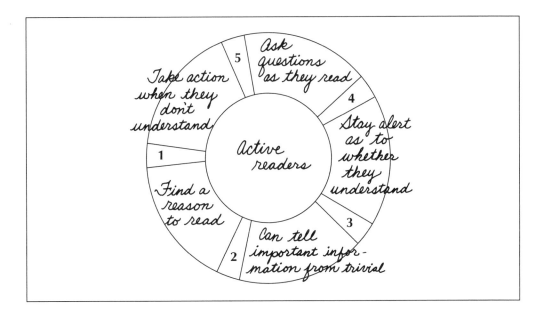

5 Ask questions as they read

Take action when they don't understand

4 Stay alert as to whether they understand

Active readers

1 Find a reason to read

3

2 Can tell important information from trivial

To check whether you're understanding what you read, and to clear up misunderstandings right away, try practicing the following techniques so that you can use them whenever you need to.

INSERT

INSERT helps you read actively because you "insert" your reactions to the text as you read it. While reading, decide whether the text confirms or contradicts what you already know. Notice what questions occur to you. Mark the text as you go along using the following symbols:

If an idea	Put this mark in the margin:
1. confirms what you thought (makes you say, "I knew that")	3
2. contradicts what you thought (makes you say, "I disagree")	X
3. is new and interesting (makes you say, "Hey, I didn't know that")	+
4. intrigues you (makes you say, "WOW! That's really neat!")	!
5. puzzles you (makes you say, "I wonder about that")	?
6. confuses you or leaves something unclear (makes you say, "I just don't understand")	??
7. strikes you as very important (makes you say, "That's really worth remembering")	*

MARK KEY
I agree = 3
I disagree = X
That's new = +
WOW = !

I wonder = ?
I don't understand = ??
That's important = *

Copy the marks and what they mean onto an index card so you can easily refer to it when using the INSERT strategy. It's possible that for some ideas, more than one notation will describe your response. If you can mark the book you're reading, go ahead and do so. If the text is borrowed, paper clip a thin strip of paper to the margin of the pages you'll be reading.

Why don't you try INSERT on a passage in this book to see how this technique works? You don't need to use all seven notations at once. You may prefer to start with one or two and gradually add more.

If you are doing INSERT when working with a partner or in a group, sharing your responses when you discuss a passage will be interesting for you.

SMART, a *S*elf-*M*onitoring *A*pproach to *R*eading and *T*hinking, will help you distinguish between what you do and don't understand. This is important because you only absorb the things you understand. SMART allows you to check yourself as you go along.

SMART

1. Read one section or paragraph at a time. As you read, place a check mark in the margin if you understand and a question mark if you don't understand.
2. After you finish reading the section, look closely at the ideas that you did not understand and do the following:
   a. Reread the parts you did not understand. If rereading clears up the misunderstanding, change the question mark to a check mark.
   b. If you are still unsure what something means, try to pinpoint the problem. Is there a word, phrase, or relationship you don't understand?
   c. Think of how you can help yourself understand. Look up a word in a dictionary or glossary, look at illustrations or diagrams in the section, review an earlier or later section of the text. If any of the strategies clears up the misunderstanding, change the question mark to a check mark.
   d. Explain to yourself exactly what you don't understand. For example, "I don't understand why dew forms." Or, "I don't understand how to program the VCR to tape shows that are on next week."

3. Study each section you read following the first two steps.
After you finish reading a section or an entire assignment,
do the following:
   a. Close the book. Tell yourself about the things you
   understand.
   b. Look back at the book to see if you forgot any
   ideas.
   c. Think about the ideas that you don't understand.
   Think about what they might mean. What can
   you do on your own to gain understanding?
   Before you ask others for help, do everything
   you can to figure it out yourself. If you do need
   to ask someone for help, be sure you can say
   exactly what you want to find out.
   d. Again, close the book again and tell yourself
   about the ideas that you do understand.

Before you read a chapter, it helps to see how the author
organized it. Preview a chapter by looking for clues on what
the chapter is about and how it's organized.

PREVIEW

How to preview a chapter:
1. Read the title.
2. Read the chapter objectives, if any.
3. Read the subheads.
4. Look at the illustrations and captions, and any other
   visual cues such as graphs, diagrams, tables, bold or
   italicized typefaces, and so on.
5. Notice how the material is organized:
   - as a problem and solution
   - as a concept
   - in sequence
   - to describe one thing
   - to compare and contrast
   - to outline a goal, action, and outcome
   - to describe conflict or cooperation
   - to describe cause and effect
   - to support a proposition

As you read, you can help yourself understand by looking back at what you've already read. By looking back at a previously read passage or chapter, you review those ideas and prepare yourself to learn more. Look-backs are helpful whether you understand or not, because you are taking the opportunity to see the material several times. Look back whenever you need or want to, so that you can make connections among the ideas you come across.

LOOK-BACKS

Another way to test your grasp of what you learn is to say out loud whatever you do or don't understand. It may help to tell someone else and ask whether you are expressing the ideas clearly. However, if you prefer, you should talk aloud to yourself. By listening to yourself think, you can tell whether or not you are sure of what you understand. As with SMART and look-backs, don't limit yourself to what you understand. Talking concisely about what you *don't* understand is important, too. Once you figure out what you don't understand, you can do something about it.

TALK-ALOUD

In Paired Reading, developed by Don Dansereau, each partner has a role. Each takes turns recalling and listening.

PAIRED READING

1. Both partners read the same section of the text. If one finishes before the other, he or she should reread the section.
2. After both finish reading, they put their books aside.
3. Without looking at the text, one partner tells the other about what he or she has read. The listener may interrupt only to ask for clarification. The listener may not add to anything the other partner says at this point.
4. When the recaller has finished, both partners should have a discussion. The listener should point out and correct misinformation and add any information that was missing.
5. The partners change roles for the next section of text and repeat until the chapter is finished.

By combining Paired Reading and SMART, you boost the power of both. Combining these activities lets you discuss with a partner what you don't understand. That way, you help each other solve problems. You realize you're not the only person who sometimes misunderstands. And you can learn

PAIRED READING
WITH SMART

new ways of solving problems by finding out how your partner does so.

1. Both partners silently read the same section of the text. As they read, they place check marks by the ideas they understand and question marks by those they don't.
2. One partner tells the other what he or she understands. They both may look back at the text whenever necessary.
3. The listener follows up by asking questions and providing any information that was left out.
4. The reteller then tells what he or she did not understand. (It's okay to look back.)
5. When possible, the listener clears up misunderstandings.
6. The listener then shares what he or she did not understand. It is now the reteller's turn to try to clear up misunderstandings.
7. As the partners explain things to one another, they go back and change any answered questions to check marks.
8. Together they make a list of questions they still need to resolve. They also decide where to go for help.
9. After all questions have been answered, the partners repeat the steps until the assignment is finished.

PAIRED QUESTIONING

This activity, developed by Joseph Vaughan and Thomas Estes, is a combination of Paired Reading and ReQuest.

1. Both partners read the chapter title or section heading and then close their books.
2. The first partner asks the second partner a question about the title or heading. The second partner answers the question as best he or she can.
3. Both partners read the first section of the text.
4. The first partner asks the second partner a question about what he or she just read. The second partner answers, looking back at the text if necessary.
5. Now the partners switch roles, with the second partner asking the questions, and the first partner answering them.
6. The first partner tells the second which ideas in the text are important and which are unimportant, and tells why he or she feels that way.
7. The second partner tells the first partner whether or not he or she agrees, and why or why not.

8. Both partners then write a summary of the section. Each partner then may read the other's summary and together write a combined summary. Or, they could summarize what they've learned in a different way—with a drawing or diagram, for example.

9. The partners go on to the next section.

Imaging is like making a movie in your head of what you read. As you read, deliberately try to form pictures in your mind. For example, if you're reading a story, try to "see" the characters and setting. That's why authors use descriptive language, analogies, and metaphors—to help evoke vivid images in a reader's mind.

IMAGING

Imaging can help not only when you read fiction but also when you read non-fiction. You can picture, for example, how tornadoes form, or how the tendons and ligaments work with your ankle joints to move your foot. If an article or text has no illustrations, try to put the information into pictures in your head. Imaging is a way to make abstract ideas become something real to you.

PARAPHRASING

Paraphrasing is putting what you read into your own words. You did this when you did paired readings and SMART. By paraphrasing what you learn, you make it easier to understand and recall what the author said. When you paraphrase, it helps to pretend that you're explaining an idea to someone else. That way, you will sum up your ideas clearly, concisely, and with details or examples. Paraphrasing goes beyond telling what the author said. You should elaborate on the author's ideas. You can deepen your understanding if you follow your paraphrasing with imaging.

THINK ABOUT WHAT YOU READ

These techniques are to studying what a warmup and workout are to your body. But one part of the workout remains. The cool-down gives your body a chance to calm down. Some fitness experts say cooling down is the most important part of the workout. You may not realize how important this concept is to studying as well. When you study, you cool down by thinking about the new ideas you now understand.

As we've said before, studying continues after you've read the assignment. To make the most of what you've read, you need a chance to reflect on what you've learned. Reflection lets you put the information together and remember what you've learned.

Here are some strategies that will help you make information you understand truly your own:

REAP

REAP, developed by Marilyn Eanet and Anthony Manzo, stands for *R*ead, *E*ncode, *A*nnotate, and *P*onder.

Read You read a selection.

Encode Write what you remember of what you've read—you can look back as often as you need to, but before you write, close the book.

Annotate Condense your retelling into a summary—decide which ideas are important enough to include in a summary and which are not. Your summary should include only the most important ideas.

Ponder Consider the importance of the ideas and compare your retelling to your summary. Ask yourself, "What do I think about that?"

Save your retelling and summary when you need to review for an exam.

"Save the Last Word for Me" is a group study technique developed by Carolyn Burke and Jerry Harste. As the group reads a selection, everyone chooses five ideas that are interesting enough to talk about. Then, everyone takes turns discussing the ideas. The person who begins saves the last word for himself or herself by saying:

"I found the statement _____ interesting. What do you think about it?" After everyone has shared his or her thoughts, the questioner tells what he or she thinks about it.

SAVE THE LAST WORD FOR ME

Turn what you've read into a poem, a story, or a journal entry. That way, you not only describe something you read, you describe how you feel about it.

FREE WRITING

In Paired Summarizing, developed by Joseph Vaughan and Thomas Estes, you and a partner work together to summarize what you've learned.

PAIRED SUMMARIZING

1. Each partner writes what he or she has read as quickly as possible without looking back at the text. (Partners fill in each other's blanks.)
2. The partners then exchange their retellings.
3. After each partner has read the other's retelling, each writes a summary of that retelling. In the summary, the partners discuss what they do and don't understand, remaining questions, and answers they have found.

Graphic organizers

Graphic organizers are special kinds of grids, outlines, or other shapes that give you a "picture" of information so that you can understand it. Just as road maps help you to plot your route when you travel, graphic organizers help you find your way to new understanding. They also help you organize different types of information so that you can understand it better. In the next few pages, you'll become familiar with some of the different types of graphic organizers that you can use.

Creating a graphic organizer is like doing a jigsaw puzzle. You need to put the pieces together to see how they form the picture. Once you have filled in your graphic organizer, you can see how the ideas tie in.

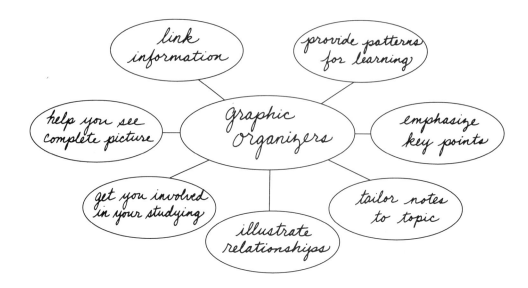

When creating a graphic organizer, you have to think about the information and decide how important it is. You simplify what you know, hear, or read into a few key words or phrases. As you figure out where each piece belongs, you judge, organize, and connect ideas. This brings you closer to what you're studying. Being involved in studying like this means you'll gain more from it. In addition, many people find that seeing information in the form of a visual pattern makes the information more meaningful to them.

In the pages that follow, eight graphic organizers have been reprinted and filled in so you can see how they work. Suggestions for types of subjects each is suitable for are also provided—each one could be useful for a number of different subjects. As each type of graphic organizer is described, ask yourself, "What topic that I'm studying now would this pattern be most helpful in organizing?" You can use some of the graphic organizers before you read and adjust them afterward. Others are more useful after you've read the materials.

At the end of this chapter, you'll find these same eight graphic organizers reprinted in blank form. You may photocopy them and use them when you study.

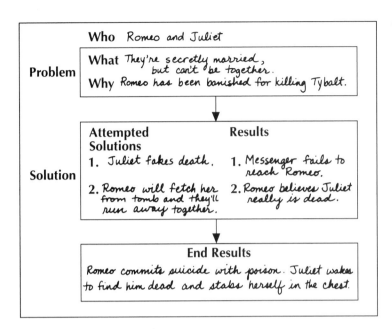

Problem/solution graphic organizers help you answer the following questions: What's the problem? Whose problem was it? What were the side effects? Was the problem solved? How was it solved? This graphic organizer is particularly helpful when studying history and literature.

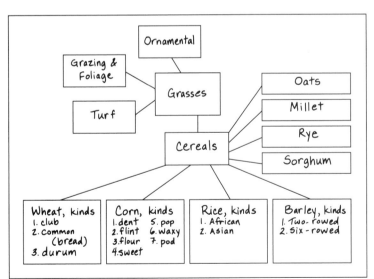

Concept graphic organizers classify information. They help you answer the following questions: What is this? What category does it belong in? How does it work? What does it do?

SEQUENCE

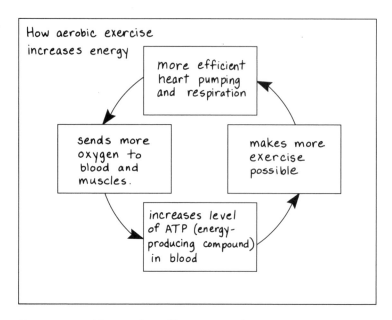

Sequence graphic organizers illustrate steps in a process, stages, or series of events that lead to a final outcome. They connect the events and the final outcome.

DESCRIPTIVE

Varieties of apples and their characteristics

	Granny Smith	Golden Delicious	Stayman	Winesap	Cortland	Empire
red			✓	✓	✓	✓
yellow		✓				
green	✓					
tart	✓		✓	✓	✓	✓
sweet		✓				
round	✓					
oval		✓				
small				✓		
medium		✓	✓	✓		
large		✓	✓		✓	✓
solid	✓	✓		✓		✓
stripes			✓		✓	
cooking	✓	✓			✓	
eating	✓	✓	✓	✓	✓	✓
processing		✓	✓	✓		

Descriptive graphic organizers describe people, places, ideas, and processes. They answer the questions: What are the features of this? When or where does this happen? How long does it take?

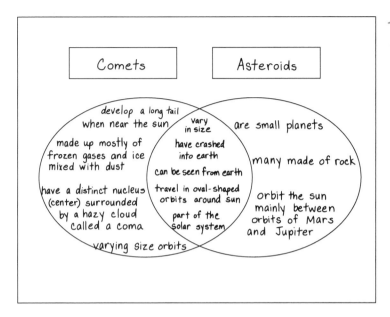

Compare/contrast graphic organizers show how things are alike and how they differ from one another. The one above is designed for two items, but you could easily design one that would be appropriate for comparing two or more items.

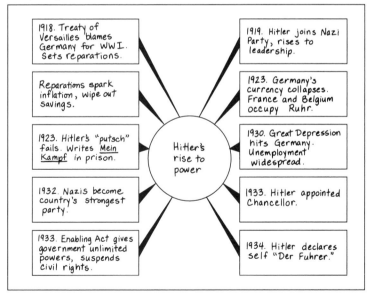

Goal/action/outcome graphic organizers answer the questions: What is the goal? What actions were taken to reach the goal? What was the outcome of those actions?

CAUSE AND EFFECT

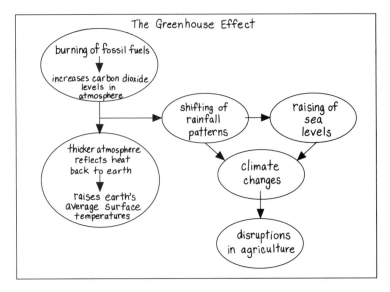

Cause-and-effect graphic organizers help you see what makes up a complex event. The questions answered are: What are the factors that caused this event? Which of those factors are most important? How do the factors relate to one another? Does what caused this event in the first place continue to do so now?

PROPOSITION/
SUPPORT

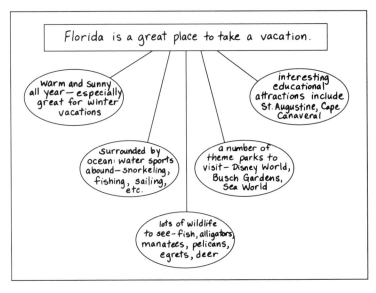

Proposition/support graphic organizers show the relationship between an idea and the statements or facts that support it. They answer questions such as: What is the generalization? How is it supported?

The graphic organizer you use should reflect the type of information you're dealing with. You can follow specific steps to decide what type to use. For example, if you wanted to make a graphic organizer of information from a chapter in a textbook, you would follow these steps:

WHICH
ORGANIZER IS
RIGHT?

1. **See how the author organized the chapter.**
   Before you read the chapter, look at the title, subheadings, illustrations and their captions, chapter objectives (if given), and chapter summary. This preview will give you an idea of the material and how it's organized. Ask yourself questions, such as: Does the author compare items or ideas? Does the chapter describe something in detail?
2. **Write down the main idea of the chapter.**
   Write one sentence summarizing what you think is the author's main point. The chapter title most likely will be your best clue. Here are some examples:

   > The author explains the process of photosynthesis.
   > The author describes the various characteristics of the hump-
   >   back whale.
   > The author lists the events that led to the Vietnam War.

3. **Ask a question.**
   For example, ask yourself: What is necessary for photosynthesis to take place? Why does photosynthesis matter? What effect does photosynthesis have on my life?
4. **Read the chapter.**
   Take notes as you read, or read the chapter aloud. Do whatever best fits your learning style. Pay particular attention to information you may have overlooked in your preview. Did reading the chapter affect your initial thoughts about the main idea? When you're finished reading, re-write your sentence on the author's main idea, if necessary. Think about your overall understanding of the chapter. Ask yourself: What were the most important points? Is anything still unclear to me? Should I reread any part of the chapter for better understanding? Do I need to do further research?
5. **Write down secondary ideas.**
   Secondary ideas are the points that help explain or support the author's main idea. Understanding these ideas is cru-

cial to understanding the main idea. Depending on the subject, you should list no more than six or seven secondary ideas. Too many will only confuse you, and the material won't be any easier for you to learn. Try to eliminate information that isn't important to the main idea.

6. **List important details under each secondary idea.**
   Be as concise as you can, and again, try to include only that material that is truly important to the main idea.

7. **Decide which graphic organizer works best.**
   Look over the graphic organizers shown on pages 119-122 and decide which one organizes information in a pattern similar to the way the author has organized the material. Different graphic organizers serve different purposes—you may have to design your own.

8. **Create your graphic organizer.**
   Using the main idea, secondary ideas, and details, fill in your graphic organizer. Make changes to the design as necessary. Don't be discouraged if you need to revise your graphic organizer before you get it right. You may find that the secondary ideas are actually the details or that your main idea was not quite right. Revisions will help you understand the information that much more.

9. **Summarize.**
   You have two choices here, based on your learning style. You can either write down a summary of the information in the graphic organizer or say it out loud. Either way, your summary should be in your own words. Why do a summary? Because it tests your overall understanding of what you've read. And it helps you identify points or facts that remain confusing.

Remember, in addition to the completed graphic organizers in this chapter, you'll find blank graphic organizers beginning on page 142. These are for you to photocopy if you'd like to use them in your studies. When using a graphic organizer, do not forget that it is crucial to pick the diagram that best matches the organization of the material you're trying to learn. And again, if a graphic organizer doesn't exactly match your subject, don't hesitate to modify the organizer. Graphic organizers are meant to help you make material easier to understand and recall. Never try to alter material to fit a graphic organizer.

Taking notes

Being able to take useful notes from lectures or written materials is a critical part of your study program. You must be able to record the essence of the ideas presented. But that can be tricky in a lecture, because you can't control how fast the information comes out of the speaker's mouth! That's why you must learn how to take notes quickly and efficiently. In the next few pages, we'll show you several different note-taking techniques, so that you can choose the strategy that best suits you and your situation.

Bring some blank graphic organizers (see pages 142-149) to a lecture or use them as you read to take notes. They are designed so that all you need to do is jot down the information in the appropriate place.

ORGANIZERS FOR NOTES

To take good notes during a lecture, you need to concentrate on what the speaker is saying, identify the major points, decide what is important, and quickly record these facts in your notebook in a well-organized way. You should sift out all unnecessary information and block out distractions. Here are some tips to help you on your way to better listening and better note-taking.

LISTENING TIPS

- First and foremost: Be prepared for the lecture. Study your assignment or the material to be covered before the lecture. This will give you a good background on the ideas the speaker plans to present. In addition, prepare questions about the material.

If you want to get even more involved, reflect on how the material in the lecture relates to you or an experience you've had. When the speaker opens the class for discussion, mention your observations. You may help others understand difficult points. When you prepare, the material becomes more meaningful, and you are in a better frame of mind to take good, concise notes.

▪ Sit in the front or center of the classroom. If you sit in the back of the room or near a door or window, your concentration will suffer. Too many distractions may occur. Chances are you'll be unable to hear the speaker, or you'll miss key points. Sitting in the front or center of the room enables you to hear better, which is critical if you learn best by listening. It also lets you clearly see materials written on the blackboard or presented on an overhead—a must for visual learners. Movies and filmstrips, too, will be easier to see and hear.

▪ Try not to tune out the lecturer. That might block learning. Sometimes, people will say something that you strongly disagree with, and you may want to stop listening. Try to concentrate on what the speaker says rather than your reaction to it.

▪ Listen for cues that indicate important ideas. Writing down every word the speaker says takes lots of time, and it clutters your notes with insignificant details. Listen carefully for cues that indicate important ideas. Does the speaker use a voice inflection to make a point stand out? Does the speaker use a topic sentence and a summary statement? Does the speaker indicate a number of important subpoints by statements such as "The three reasons . . ." or "A list of five . . ."? Does the speaker repeat important statements, or say things such as, "Listen carefully to this point"? All these cues help you record important ideas.

▪ Be ready to ask questions. Sometimes, the speaker will set aside time for discussion. Ask questions that will help clarify any points you missed or don't understand.

▪ Use shortcuts in note-taking. It's a good idea to create your own form of shorthand for note-taking. Begin by shortening one or two words that you frequently use in taking notes. Add a few words to your list each week.

Some words you will use only in one class for one or two lectures. In these cases, make a note at the beginning of a day's notes, indicating what certain abbreviations mean. Remember to make your abbreviations clear enough so that they will not be mistaken for other words. Can you identify each of the following abbreviations? The vowels have been left out of each word.

pplr	popular
hmsphr	hemisphere
tmbr	timber
cttl	cattle
qn	queen

Another way to shorten words is to use the beginning of a word to stand for the whole word. For example:

add	address
biol	biology
soc st	social studies
math	mathematics
sci	science

Long words are usually easier to abbreviate than short words. Keep in mind that the reason you're using abbreviations and symbols is to make note-taking quicker and easier. Choose shortcuts that are simple to remember. Then, get in the habit of using these shortcuts.

■ Write down the examples given in the lecture. The speaker will probably use examples to clarify particular points. Include the examples in your notes. They will increase your understanding of the main idea. They also will serve as reminders of the underlying principles when you review.

■ Review your lecture notes. Most notes need editing to make them more useful. Well-organized notes improve your ability to remember what you learn in a lecture. Review and reorganize your notes the same day they are taken, if possible.

■ If you have trouble taking notes, tune out distractions by focusing on a single sound. For example, next time you're in a crowded place, try to focus on just one of the many sounds you hear: one person's voice, a train in the background, background music, and so on. This will give you practice in concentrating better.

■ While listening to two minutes of a lecture, write down five key words to help you focus on the main idea.

■ Learn to recognize voice emphasis in sentences; emphasized phrases provide keys for understanding content.

■ Learn to become aware of pitch, tempo, and rhythm; say

Abbreviations and symbols

a.k.a.	also known as	long.	longitude
a.m.	ante meridiem (morning)	mag.	magazine
		mdse.	merchandise
amt.	amount	-	minus
&	and	min.	minute
ans.	answer	misc.	miscellaneous
bib.	bibliography	mo.	month
bldg.	building	mph	miles per hour
ch.	chapter	neg.	negative
dept.	department	no. or #	number
diam.	diameter	opp.	opposite
div.	division	p.	page
$	dollars	pd.	paid
doz.	dozen	%	percent
ea.	each	pkg.	package
ed.	edition	pl.	plural
e.g.	*exempli gratia* (for example)	+	plus
		pop.	population
=	equals	pp.	pages
et al.	et alii (and others)	pres.	president
etc.	et cetera	recd.	received
ex.	example	ref.	referee, reference
fem.	feminine	RR	railroad
fig.	figure	sci.	science
freq.	frequency	sing.	singular
ft.	foot	sq.	square
govt.	government	subj.	subject
>	is greater than	tel.	telephone
≥	is greater than or equal to	USA	United States of America
hosp.	hospital	vocab.	vocabulary
hr.	hour	vol.	volume
ht.	height	vs.	versus
i.e.	*id est* (that is)	w/	with
illus.	illustration	wk.	week
incl.	including	w/o	without
intro.	introduction	wt.	weight
lat.	latitude	yd.	yard
<	is less than	yr.	year
≤	is less than or equal to		

the same sentence while varying each of these qualities so you will be better able to hear and interpret them.

PRACTICE

Listen carefully to a news report on the radio. When the program is over, write down all the major news items you remember from the broadcast.

If you're part of a club or attend meetings regularly, take notes during a meeting. When the meeting is over, check your notes with the appointed secretary of the group to see how your notes compare.

SQ3R

SQ3R stands for *Survey-Question-Read-Recite-Review*, which are the steps that readers follow when they use this method. SQ3R really is worth trying.

Survey. You begin with the letter S, which stands for survey. Get a good idea of the chapter's content before diving in headfirst. Survey the title, the introduction, the summary, pictures and maps, chapter questions, headings, subheadings, and words in special print (**boldface**, *italics*, or ALL CAPITAL LETTERS).

Textbooks are usually written from well-organized outlines. The main points of the outline are generally used as the headings. Headings are important clues to the contents of a chapter. If you use the chapter's headings and subheadings as an outline for your notes, you will have the skeleton of your notes completed before you even begin reading the chapter. For example, in a chapter discussing the Revolutionary War in America, these headings might appear:

> The Causes of the War
> Events Leading to the Revolution
> The First Battles

Question. After you've carefully surveyed the material, change all the headings into questions. Questions help you learn because to find the answers, you need to read actively. Questions challenge you and give you a purpose for trying to master material.

This technique may seem difficult for you at first. But you will find that it gets easier with practice. For example, as you read a chapter on the Revolutionary War, change the headings into questions.

What were the main causes of the Revolutionary War?
What was happening in America before the Revolutionary
    War broke out?
What were the names of the first battles?

These questions serve as your guide to study. You'll find that questions usually tip you off as to what the author considers to be the important points. Under each of the headings, subheadings often appear. For example:

> The first battles
>   Men under arms
>   War leaders
>   Battlefronts

Turn subheadings into questions, as well. For example:

> Who were the soldiers who fought in the war?
> Who were the war leaders of each side?
> Where were the first battles fought?

Write a list of all your questions, and keep them in the same order that the headings appear in the book. Be sure to leave enough space on your paper after each question for answers, which you will fill in later. It might help you to keep all these questions in a notebook (your three-ring binder, if you have chosen to use that system). With a framework of questions, you are ready to go on to the next step.

Read. Read your assignment. Read thoroughly and carefully. As you read, remember: You have a list of questions waiting to be answered. See page 107 for a strategy that will help you tap into what you already know and check on how well you're understanding.

You undoubtedly will run across illustrations, such as charts, diagrams, and figures, as you read. Don't overlook these important sources of information. These elements usually help support the material in the text. You often will find that you understand something better after you examine related illustrations or charts. In your notes, make a note of the figure or chart and what page it's on, and write one or two sentences describing it. Most likely, it will have a caption from which you can generate your notes; but use your own words so that you're recording how you understand the concept.

As you continue to read, make note of definitions of key words. Learning new words is a major part of studying and learning. Most textbooks highlight important, new, or difficult words in some way. They often will appear printed in either boldface or italics.

The term may be defined for you within the text, or a glossary of terms may be included somewhere in the book. If your textbook does not use these features, you will need to define the words for yourself, usually by looking them up in a dictionary (another reason to keep one handy). You may find that this extra effort will help you better understand and remember the new words you've learned.

When defining words for your notes, put the definition in your own words and draw "pictures," if appropriate. Again, this will help you understand and remember them. If you find that looking up words breaks your concentration, then make a list of unfamiliar words and look them up when you have finished reading. However, if an unfamiliar word is essential to the meaning of a passage, you should look it up right away.

Recite. Once you read a section, stop and describe in your own words the major ideas that were presented. Since textbooks are divided into sections with headings and subheadings, recite whenever you reach one of these convenient stopping places. Take in only as many sections as you think you can absorb in a study session. Remember: Any kind of heading is a clue that a new concept or idea is being presented.

In your own words, and without looking at the book, recite the main idea and the answers to the questions you wrote. Then, write down your answers, giving examples as necessary. Draw diagrams or use a graphic organizer, if they help. If you have trouble answering a question, go back, reread the section, and try again.

When you're ready to move on to the next section, repeat the process: Read to answer the questions, then look away from the book, recite the main ideas and answers to the questions before writing the answers. Continue this way until you complete the reading assignment.

Review. You are now at the final step of SQ3R. You are ready to go back over the material and review it. Survey again what you have read. Skim over the headings of the chapter, ask yourself what they mean and what information they contain. Recite the important ideas under each heading. Answer any questions you haven't yet answered. Reread if you cannot answer a question without looking at the book or your notes. Your review should include studying your notes and making comments as necessary to help clarify them.

Finally, do the activities and answer the end-of-chapter questions in your textbook. Also remember to review any class notes at this time. Keep all your notes—from class and the textbook—carefully filed for future reviews. The material will be invaluable when you study for tests.

Reviewing is not something you should do only at the end of a chapter or before taking an examination. Do it as often as you can—during free-study times—so you don't forget what you've worked so hard to learn.

OUTLINING

The traditional method for organizing information is outlining. You can use outlining to take notes from either a book or a lecture. Many speakers write their lectures from an outline, so they present the material in that format.

Often, speakers post their outlines on bulletin boards or distribute them before the lecture. This is a good opportunity to either photocopy the outline or copy it on a separate sheet of paper, leaving a generous amount of space between headings. If you don't have time to copy the entire outline before the lecture begins, record the information in the outline form as the speaker discusses the topic. Sometimes, the photocopy itself is a good place to jot notes.

Just as books give you clues as to what is important by using titles, subheadings, and different type faces, lecturers let you know what is important, too. They also give titles and subheadings, and define key words and phrases. But they also indicate the importance of different points by varying their tone of voice. Listen to how a lecturer's voice rises and falls to emphasize the most important information. Sometimes, lecturers tell you outright, "This is an important idea. Be sure you get this down in your notes." They may also guide you by saying something like, "I'll speak about this in greater detail later." That way, you know to write down the idea and leave enough room to fill in the details when the lecturer returns to the topic.

The following example shows how to organize an outline:

The outline format

Roman numeral

I. First main idea of the topic you are outlining

capital letter

    A. Subtopic supporting this idea

numeral

        1. Important fact relating to A

lower-case letters

            a. Detail supporting 1

            b. Second detail supporting 1

lower-case
Roman numeral

               (i) Minor detail supporting b

               (ii) Another minor detail supporting b

        2. Another important fact relating to A

    B. Another subtopic supporting the first main idea

        1. Important fact relating to B
        2. Another important fact relating to B

II. Second main idea of the topic you are outlining

    A. Subtopic

    B. Subtopic

    C. Subtopic

III. Third main idea of the topic you are outlining

    A. Subtopic

    B. Subtopic

Note that each subdivision always has two or more headings in it. The different subdivisions are indented to show their relative importance. How detailed you make an outline depends on your topic and the purpose of your outline. Be careful not to make your outline so detailed that it becomes a lengthy summary that takes a long time to read and understand.

You can write the various headings of your outline in phrases or short sentences. Sometimes, minor headings can be just a single word. The order of the points on your outline should be in some logical pattern. Outlines often have a chronological order, in which items are listed from earliest to most recent dates. When it comes to outlining a book or a speech, you should always follow the author's or speaker's subdivisions of chapters, topics, or main points.

LOOKING AT
OUTLINES

You can find many excellent examples of outlines in encyclopedias. Below is an outline from an encyclopedia article on leaves. Note how all the main ideas are tied together and how easy it is to distinguish between the main ideas and the subtopics supporting them.

Leaves

I. The importance of leaves

II. The life story of a leaf
    A. A leaf begins its life
    B. The leaf becomes fully grown
    C. The leaf changes color
    D. The leaf dies

III. The parts of a leaf
    A. The blade
    B. The petiole
    C. The stipules

IV. How a leaf makes food
    A. Obtaining raw materials
    B. Photosynthesis
    C. Transpiration

V. Specialized leaves
    A. Protective leaves
    B. Storage leaves
    C. Tendrils
    D. Bracts
    E. Insect-capturing leaves

VI. How to collect leaves
    A. How to preserve leaves
    B. How to make leaf rubbings and prints

Don't you think this outline, with some added detail under each subtopic, would help you review for a test or for writing a paper on leaves? You probably would not have to reread the original material if you outlined the material properly.

Suppose you are writing a paper on the pollution of Lake Michigan, and you have compiled the following list of important ideas. How would you arrange them into an outline that shows the main ideas (I, II, etc.) and subtopics (A, B, etc.)?

TEST YOUR
OUTLINING SKILL

The Pollution of Lake Michigan

Main idea: Because Lake Michigan is extensively polluted, only strong laws will provide an effective solution.
The causes of pollution
Sewage-treatment regulations

Solutions to the problem
Pesticides used for farming
Increased cost of water purification
Undesirable levels of algae
Evidence of pollution
Industrial wastes
Maximum water-temperature regulation
Thermal pollution from nuclear energy plants
Pesticide controls
Contaminated fish
Poorly treated sewage
Laws limiting industrial wastes

Once you've finished writing your outline based on this list, compare it to the one below and see how you did. Note that the subtopics (A, B, etc.) could be given in any order.

I. Evidence of pollution
    A. Contaminated fish
    B. Increased cost of water purification
    C. Undesirable levels of algae

II. The causes of pollution
    A. Industrial wastes
    B. Pesticides used for farming
    C. Poorly treated sewage
    D. Thermal pollution from nuclear energy plants

III. Solutions to the problem
    A. Laws limiting industrial wastes
    B. Pesticide controls
    C. Sewage-treatment regulations
    D. Maximum water-temperature regulation

The secret to good outlining is finding the main ideas and connecting them properly. The more outlines you make, the better your outlines will become. If you find that outlining works for you—that it fits your learning style—get into the habit of outlining material whenever you study.

THE CORNELL SYSTEM

The Cornell system of note-taking was developed by Walter Pauk at Cornell University. To use it, you have to remember the five R's: record, reduce, recite, reflect, and review.

1. Record

Draw a vertical line down your paper. The left side of your page should be one-third the width of the paper, the right side two-thirds. Jot down notes on the right side of the line.

2. Reduce

Use the column on the left side of the line to "reduce" your notes to key words and phrases that describe the most important information you need to remember.

3. Recite

Fold back or cover the note-taking column. With only the key words showing, read each one in turn and recite anything that you understand or remember about the concept.

4. Reflect

Take a break. When you get back to work, think about the information in your notes without looking back at them. State what you do and don't understand about the topic. Decide how you are going to clear up any misunderstandings and do it.

5. Review

Review your notes at regular intervals so that you stay familiar with the information that they contain.

Whales	
Reduce	Note-taking
sea	huge animals that live in the sea
mammals	look similar to fish, but warm-blooded
smart	whales are intelligent
largest	blue whale largest animal on earth (100 feet long, 100 short tons)
smaller	not all whales are enormous (narwhals and belugas 10-15 ft.)

LISTS

Simply listing the central ideas of your material may work for you. Write down one idea on each line. Skip a line or two between ideas. Then, when you're done, organize the information in a way that makes sense to you.

If you prefer highlighting to taking notes, do so using the principles of note-taking. Students often highlight too much. Only highlight the important ideas and details and key words and phrases with their definitions. First, read a passage and think about it. Then go back and highlight. If you highlight thoughtfully, you can reread the highlighted parts for a good review of important facts and ideas. Use a special highlighing marker. Colored pens and ordinary markers tend to be messy.

The material you choose to highlight depends on which facts are most important for you to learn. If you find highlighting helps you, highlight key points in your outlines or notes as you prepare for tests. This will cut the amount of material you have to review before the exam.

SPECIALIZED
VOCABULARY

Every subject has words that help describe it. Think about words you use in math, such as *ratio, quotient, multiple;* in science, such as *viscosity, hypothesis, theory;* and in geology, such as *anticline, igneous*, and *tectonic plate*. You must understand the vocabulary of a particular subject to understand its ideas. Using the specific vocabulary of a subject is the most clear and concise way experts have to explain something. Once you know the vocabulary of a subject, you can speak fluently in its "language."

MASTERING NEW
WORDS

Follow these guidelines to learn new vocabulary:
1. Choose one word at a time. Ask yourself:
   a. What do I know about this word already?
   b. What ideas or things do I associate with this word?
   c. What do I think it means?
2. Answer the following questions to find out about the word and examine its history:
   a. What words have similar meanings?
   b. Where does this word come from?
   c. What part of speech is this word? Is it a noun, verb, adjective, or adverb?
3. How would you use this word? To inform, explain, express emotion, describe, or label?

Reports and projects

Your best tool for tackling reports and projects is *planning*. Good planning allows you to break down a large or complicated project into manageable segments. It also helps you to stay focused on your assignment and avoid a last-minute "rush" to finish on time.

Here is a good step-by-step plan that you can use for preparing most any type of long-term assignment:

- Identify your topic and the requirements of the assignment. Ask questions if necessary. You should come up with at least two or three ideas in case one doesn't work.

- Make preliminary notes on each of your ideas.

- Do a library search. What information is available on each topic? What research has been done on it lately? You may find very little information on one of the topics. This may mean you should avoid it. Based on your research, make a final decision of your topic.

- Write an outline or use a graphic organizer to plan the flow of ideas. If you do an outline, use the format shown on page 133.

- If you're writing a paper or preparing an oral report, write a first draft. Even if you are doing a project, you often will need to prepare a short paper explaining it.

- Revise your paper, speech, or project as necessary. Maybe something doesn't sound right or doesn't work as you thought it would. Be sure to do this step well in advance of your due date. You need time to make mistakes and find solutions.

- Prepare your final product. Review the requirements of the assignment one last time. Be sure you've included everything.

For preparing a research paper or any other type of composition, these guidelines will help you improve your writing:

WRITING SPECIFICS

1. Define your central theme or idea clearly.
2. Locate source materials.
3. Develop an outline and follow it.
4. Gather information.

When you take notes for a paper or project, you will be reading and gathering information from many different sources. For this reason, it is a good idea to use 3-by-5-inch index cards. You can rearrange these cards more easily than

sheets of paper, so they're easier to keep organized. Make sure you put down such information as the source, author, and page number at the top of each card.

Always thoroughly read your sources before you start taking notes. Be selective. Do not copy unimportant details or information you can easily remember. Write only summary sentences or factual material, such as statistics, that will be important to your report or term paper. If you are going to use a direct quote, make sure you copy it word-for-word. Remember, always use quotation marks. Never rewrite a quote in your own words. However, if you decide to leave out part of a quotation, write three spaced dots (. . .), called an ellipsis, to show where words, phrases, or sentences were left out.

Put each new idea on a separate card. Your cards will be easier to rearrange and organize later, when you begin to draft your paper. Be sure to put information from different sources on separate cards, even if they say the same thing about the same subject.

5. Write a first draft. At this point, don't worry about punctuation and spelling. Just write down your ideas. This is where you'll see if your outline makes sense. Revise it as necessary.

6. Revise your paper, working toward making it final.

7. Proofread your finished paper. Check for spelling errors by reading your paper backward, word-by-word. This method guarantees that you actually read each individual word. Ask someone else to proofread your paper. Other readers often see things you've overlooked.

If you're doing an oral report, remember three words: practice, practice, practice. You'll have an easier time if you:

- Organize your presentation the same way you would a written report.
- Be creative. Try to think of attention-getting openers and memorable closers. Include examples, stories, jokes, and fascinating facts. Make your presentation visually appealing by including charts, graphs, pictures, or videos.
- If it's permitted, use note cards to help you remember your facts. Make the notes short and clean so you'll be able to refer to them easily.
- Practice in front of a mirror, with your parents, or with some friends or classmates.
- Dress the part—appearances count.

A bibliography is a list of the sources you used to prepare your report or term paper—books, magazine articles, pamphlets, interviews, and so on. It should include only those sources that you actually used in the final report, not those you consulted but disregarded. The purpose of the bibliography is to tell the reader where you got your information and where the reader could get additional information.

Bibliography entries should provide information about the title, author, publishers, and publication date of any source. Entries for articles include the page numbers for the complete article. The entries are listed in alphabetical order according to the authors' last names. Entries with no author are inserted alphabetically according to the first word of the title (disregarding *a, an,* and *the*). In general, bibliography entries are not numbered.

Here is a sample bibliography you can use as a guide:

Bedini, Silvio A. *Thomas Jefferson: Statesman of Science.* Macmillan, 1990.

McLaughlin, Jack. *Jefferson and Monticello: The Biography of a Builder.* Henry Holt, 1988.

Thomas Jefferson: A Reference Biography. Ed. by Merrill D. Peterson. Scribner, 1986.

Wernick, Robert. "At Monticello, a big birthday for the former owner." *Smithsonian,* May 1993, pp. 80-92.

Problem/Solution Graphic Organizer

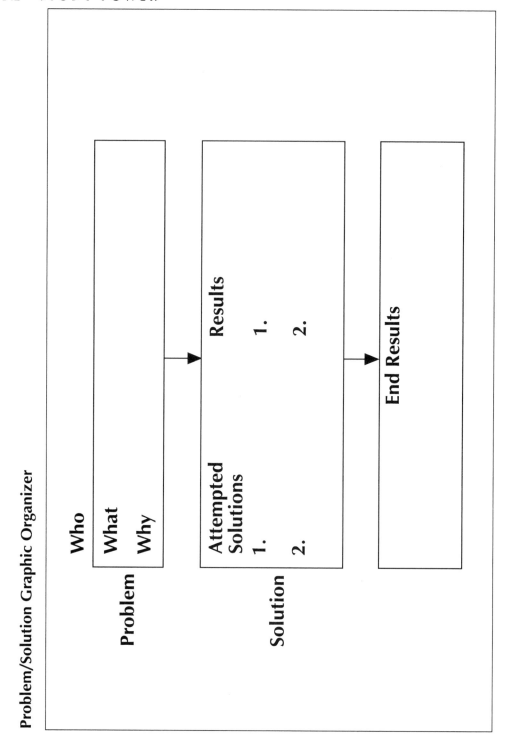

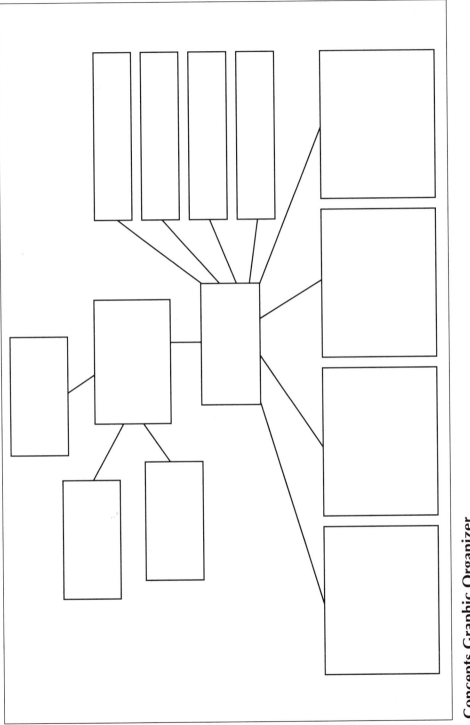

Concepts Graphic Organizer

Sequences Graphic Organizer

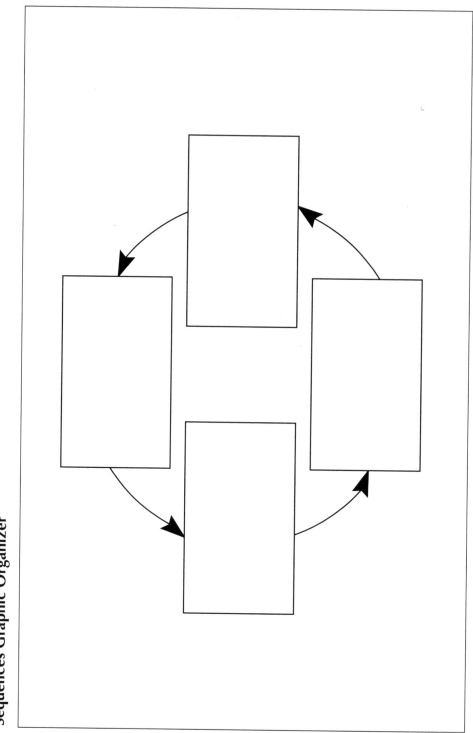

Descriptive Graphic Organizer

Compare/Contrast Graphic Organizer

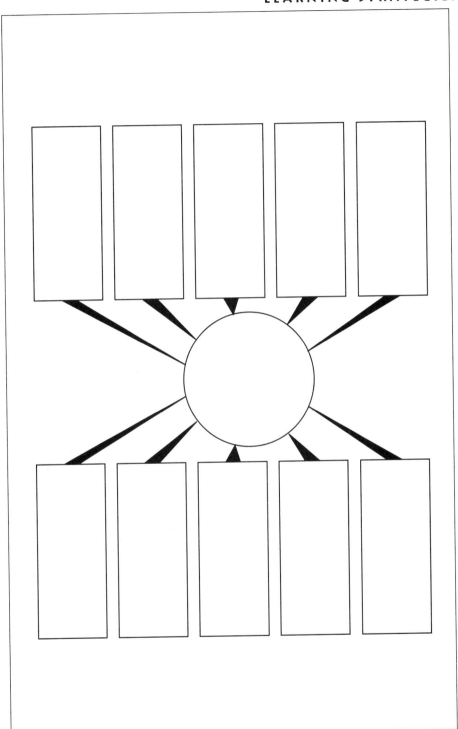

Goal/Action/Outcome Graphic Organizer

Cause-and-Effect Graphic Organizer

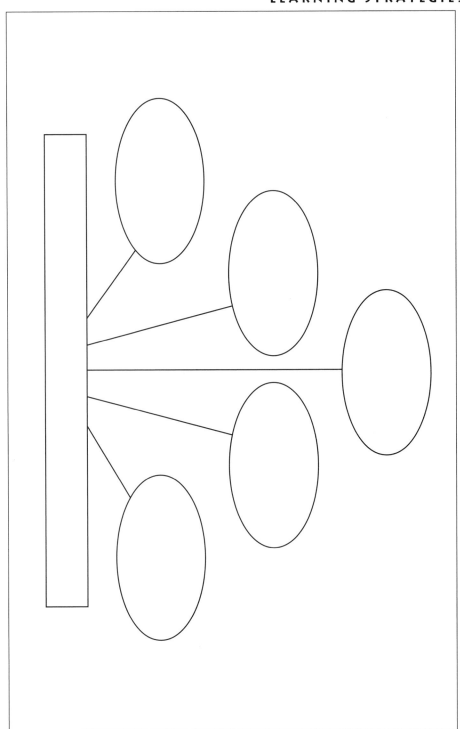

Proposition/Support Graphic Organizer

✎ Reference books ✎ Dictionaries ✎ Thesauruses

✎ Encyclopedias ✎ Atlases ✎ Almanacs

✎ Books about information ✎ Judging sources

✎ The public library ✎ Other resources

✎ Information is everywhere

You get information from many sources and in many forms. A friend may call to ask, "Did you hear who was elected President?" and proceed to tell you. You can read, listen to, or watch the news to make sure your friend was correct. Maybe you predicted the outcome of the race ahead of time and are using these sources of information to confirm your hunch. You can be sure that weekly news magazines will carry the newly elected President's photo on their covers and details of the election inside. Bookstores will stock hot-off-the-press campaign memoirs and biographies of the new President. Some of the books may be available on audiotape, too. And don't forget television specials. During the election, someone was busy pulling together newsreel footage, interviewing the candidates' former teachers and neighbors, and taking a walk through their hometowns. Those TV specials may become part of a video series on presidents that you can rent or buy.

Oceans of information are available on any subject, in many formats: books, magazines, audio- and videotapes, TV talk shows, radio discussions, computer programs, and the old-fashioned approach known as word-of-mouth. Sometimes, the sheer volume of information can seem overwhelming. You could get dizzy thinking about how much there is to know and the many places to find it. Not only do you need to know where to get the most reliable information, you need to know how to get it. After all, if you have a resource but you don't know how to use it, you can't get the information from the source to your brain.

This period of history is called the Information Age, perhaps because so much new information is being discovered, compiled, and published. An industry known as "information technology" has been born because we need to know how to get information and how to keep up with it.

Reference books

The types of reference books you can choose from are almost as varied and wide-ranging as the subjects they cover. Some reference sources provide only bare facts. These let the information speak for itself. For example, statistics often are presented with little or no comment.

Other reference books, such as a desk encyclopedia, include a short paragraph or two about the subjects covered. Still others cover a limited number of topics but provide detailed or specialized information on those topics. Dictionaries, encyclopedias, atlases, and almanacs, for example, contain information in different depth and detail.

FINDING
INFORMATION

When you need to look up something, you can decide where to turn to only if you know what sources are available, what kind of information they contain, and how much detail they provide. At times, you simply want to know a fact without having to weed through pages and pages of explanation. For example, if you need to know the value of houses in your area, you don't want an account of the county's entire history. You should choose a source that presents the information in the exact way you want it. In this case, you need a list of your county's statistics. In addition to knowing what kind of source you need, you must know where to find it. You'll probably find statistical data for your area at your city's department of records and your local library.

You probably already are familiar with many types of reference books. Many people have at least one dictionary in their home, classroom, or office. Also, you're likely to find an encyclopedia, thesaurus, and atlas on many home, office, and classroom bookshelves. That's because the information these books contain is used regularly, sometimes several times a day. It would be extremely inconvenient to have to run to the library every time you needed to look up a spelling. Having these books on hand means that you can get answers to some questions right away.

Specialized references, such as law dictionaries, medical encyclopedias, association directories, and United Nations abstracts, may be less familiar to you than dictionaries or encyclopedias, but they are just as useful. Because you're likely to use these books less often than you would a dictionary, it may not make sense to have them at home. Schools often have a number of reference books on hand so that students can find information they need easily. Some workplaces may stock a variety of references as well.

To find a large, up-to-date collection of reference books, you should turn to your local library. Try visiting the library to see firsthand what it offers. You even can arrange to take a guided tour. A librarian would be the best person to walk you through the reference room. To prepare you for your visit, we will give you a brief introduction to some of the types of references published.

Reference books are tools, and like any tool, they are designed for a specific purpose. Just as people use bread knives for slicing bread, carving knives for cutting meat, and table knives for spreading mayonnaise, they use specialized reference books for finding different types of information. While a dictionary definition may provide a few facts about a topic, an encyclopedia article will give more detailed information. If you simply wanted to know how to spell a word, how to divide it into syllables, or how to pronounce it, a dictionary would be the ideal source. On the other hand, what if you wanted to know who holds the record for most major-league strikeouts? It might take a while to find the answer in a general encyclopedia if you had to leaf through many articles. It's easier to find sports statistics in an almanac.

Where to find what you need

Information needed	Reference book
Words	Dictionary
General	Encyclopedia
Geographical	Atlas
Statistical	Almanac
How-to	Handbook on a specific topic
People	Biographical dictionary
Names and addresses	Directory
Books and materials	Bibliography

Dictionaries

Basically, two kinds of dictionaries exist: general and specialized. General dictionaries range in size from small pocket dictionaries to large multivolume or tabletop books. Some dictionaries are now on computer software. A general dictionary contains information on everyday words.

You may not need all the information given in more special-

A general dictionary tells you:

- How a word is used
- As what part or parts of speech a word can be used
- What forms the word can take
- Examples of how a word is used in a sentence
- How to pronounce a word
- How to break a word into syllables
- What the individual parts of a word mean
- The origin of a word or phrase

What a dictionary tells you

In addition to defining words, a dictionary provides much useful information about them. You can get the most out of a dictionary by learning what its abbreviations and symbols stand for. These examples come from *The World Book Dictionary*.

Word entries begin in bold black type. Only proper nouns are capitalized. The first letter of the entry extends into the margin for easy location. This dictionary uses an asterisk to indicate that the entry is accompanied by an illustration.

Illustrations clarify the definitions. Labels show which meaning of the word is illustrated.

Pronunciations are given in phonetic symbols. This dictionary has a key to its phonetic symbols at the bottom of each right-hand page, with more detailed information at the front of the book.

Parts of speech labels show the word's grammatical use. Any word used as more than one part of speech is defined accordingly. The parts of speech are abbreviated, as in *adj.* for *adjective* and *n* for *noun*. Verbs are shown as transitive (*v.t.*) or intransitive (*v.i.*).

Phrases that include the key word but have special meanings of their own are explained separately.

Synonyms that have the same or nearly the same meaning as the defined words appear immediately after the definition.

Synonym studies explain in detail the various shades of meaning of some synonyms. All these studies include examples.

Usage notes explain points of spelling or grammar and advise how to use the word in speaking or writing.

* ab.do.man (ab′də man, ab dō′·), *n.* **1a** the part of the body containing the stomach and the intestines; belly. In man and other mammals the abdomen is a large cavity between the chest (thorax) and the pelvis, and also contains the liver, pancreas, kidneys, and spleen. **b** a corresponding region in vertebrates below mammals. **2** the last of the three parts of the body of insects and many other arthropods, including spiders and crustaceans. [< Latin *abdōmen*]

* abdomen definition 2

abdomen   thorax   head

ab·dom·i·nal (ab dom′ə nəl), *adj.* of the abdomen; in the abdomen; for the abdomen. *Bending the body exercises the abdominal muscles.* **syn** ventral, visceral. — **ab·dom′i·nal·ly**, *adv.*
abdominal brain, solar plexus.
ab·dom·i·nous (ab dom′ə nəs), *adj.* potbellied.
a·bide¹ (ə bīd′), *v.*, **a·bode** or **a·bid·ed**, **a·bid·ing**. — *v.t.* **1** To put up with; endure; tolerate. *A good housekeeper can't abide dust. She can't abide him* **syn** bear, stand. **2** to await submissively; submit to; sustain. *He must abide his fatal doom* (Joanna Baillie). **3** to await defiantly; withstand. *He soon learned to abide... terrors which most of my bolder companions shrank from encountering* (Hugh Miller). **4** *Archaic.* to wait for; await. *I will abide the coming of my lord* (Tennyson). — *v.i.* **1** to stay; remain; wait. *Abide with me for a time. I'll call upon you straight. abide within* (Shakespeare). *He within his ships abode the while* (William Cowper). **2** to continue to live (in a place); reside; dwell. *No martin there in winter shall abide* (John Dryden). **3** to continue (in some state or action). *ye shall abide in my love* (John 15 10). **4** to continue in existence; endure. *Thou hast established the earth, and it abideth* (Psalms 119 90). **syn** last, Archaic, to be left. **6** *Obsolete.* to stay behind.
abide by, a to accept and follow out; be bound by. *Both teams will abide by the umpire's decision.* **b** to remain faithful to; stand firm by; be true to; fulfill. *Abide by your promise.*
a·bil·i·ty (ə bil′ə tē), *n.*, *pl.* **-ties.** **1** the power to do or act; the ability to think clearly. *The old horse still has the ability to work* **syn** capability, capacity. **2** skill. *Washington had great ability as a general.* **3** power to do some special thing; natural gift; talent. *Musical ability often shows itself early in life.* [< Middle French *habilité*, learned borrowing from Latin *habilitās* aptness < *habilis* able]
— *Syn.* **2, 3 Ability, talent** mean special power to do or for doing something. **Ability** applies to a demonstrated physical or mental power to do a certain thing. *She has developed unusual ability as a dancer.* **Talent** applies to an inborn capacity for doing a special thing. *a child with a remarkable talent for painting.*
► After **ability** the infinitive of a verb preceded by *to* is used, rather than the gerund preceded by *of:* *a lawyer needs the ability to think clearly, not of thinking clearly.* The preposition used after *ability* and before a noun is *in: ability in music.*
A·bim·e·lech (ə bim′ə lek), *n.* a son of Gideon who was set up as king of Israel by the people of Shechem (in the Bible; Judges 9).
ab init., ab initio.
ab in·i·ti·o (ab′ i nish′ē ō), *Latin.* from the beginning. *The decree was not a nullity in the sense of being void ab initio* (London Times).

Definitions give the precise meanings of words. If a word has more than one meaning, the definitions are numbered. This dictionary lists the most common meanings first. Some dictionaries present definitions in historical order, with the earliest meanings first.

Examples point out how the word is used in phrases or sentences.

Cross-references show that the form consulted is less widely used than some other form, which has its own main entry.

Other forms of the word include the principal parts of verbs, unusual plural forms, and comparative forms for adjectives.

Quotations from well-known authors or publications illustrate the meaning of the word. The sources of quotations are identified.

Usage labels, such as *Slang, Informal, Archaic,* and *Obsolete,* indicate when and where the word is acceptable in current English usage. Each label is defined in a list at the front of the dictionary.

Etymologies tell what language or languages a word comes from, usually with its meaning in the original language. The symbol < means *comes from*.

Foreign words and phrases in common use in English have entries that give their pronunciation and translation, often with examples or illustrative quotations.

ized dictionaries. There are all kinds of dictionaries, and they differ in the depth of coverage they give each word. Choose the dictionary that most suits your needs.

If you want to know where curious expressions and slang come from, turn to dictionaries that specialize in colloquial sayings. If want to know the history of a word, you'll find an etymological dictionary helpful. There's even a dictionary on computer that will help you solve crossword puzzles by giving you all the words of a certain pattern. For example, if you know the word is *br_ _k,* the computer dictionary will tell you it's either *break, brick, brink, brisk,* or *brook.* Dictionaries on computer even can help you find a word when you know its meaning, but you can't think of the word itself. If you enjoy tracing word histories or want to know exactly how many definitions the word *good* has, you'll be able to find a dictionary to suit you.

The reference area of the library has many specialized dictionaries. It has rhyming dictionaries to help you write poems; science dictionaries of technical terms for biology, chemistry, and physics; chronologies and dictionaries of world history with short entries on events and cultural trends; and biographical dictionaries that contain short articles about people. You will most likely be able to find a dictionary that specializes in any particular topic, from the arts to zoology.

Look in the front of any dictionary to find out what information it contains and how it is organized. Also check the key abbreviations, codes, and symbols the dictionary uses. And don't forget that definitions can vary somewhat from one dictionary to another.

Thesauruses

Have you ever found yourself using the same word over and over again in a paper or report? Many words are so common and familiar that you find yourself choosing them, in conversation or writing, without thinking twice. You may not even notice how often you use a particular word until someone points it out to you. A thesaurus is a reference book that can help you vary your language.

Sometimes you know you can use a more powerful or interesting word to describe something or express an emotion, but you can't quite put your finger on it. That's when you should turn to a thesaurus. A thesaurus is a book of synonyms (words that have similar meanings) and antonyms (words that have opposite meanings).

Most of the reports, stories, poems, and essays you write will be read by someone else. Your writing is a record of what you think about something and how you think about it. Therefore, you should strive to express your thoughts clearly.

The first rule of good writing is, "Show, don't tell." Read the following sentence and the list of words from a thesaurus to see how the sentence can become more vivid:

> Having been cooped up for hours, the children ran (dashed, bolted, shot, sped, scampered, flew) out of the house.

Which word would you substitute for the word *ran*? Wouldn't any one of these alternatives show the reader more than the word *ran*?

A thesaurus gives you a variety of word choices. A note of caution, however: Be sure that you understand the meaning of the word you choose. If you don't, you could end up using a

word that doesn't say what you intend. You may sound phony if you choose a word that's too formal or old-fashioned. Remember, the longest word isn't always the best.

Some thesauruses are organized like dictionaries. Others are like indexes: You look up the word in the back to find which section deals with it. Many word-processing programs have a thesaurus built in. Thesauruses also differ in the number of words they provide. Look through several to find the type of thesaurus that suits your needs. Some thesauruses may have separate sections on particular subjects, such as science, to help you find specialized words for that subject. Other features thesauruses may include are idioms (expressions unique to a language), quotes, phrases, slang, foreign words and phrases, and colloquialisms (informal expressions). The best thesaurus is the one you feel most comfortable using.

Encyclopedias

An encyclopedia is like a small library. It gives you information on topics in many fields of knowledge. When you need to know about the former Soviet republics, the state bird of Wyoming, or the first airplane ever built, go first to a general encyclopedia. For example, an article on radar tells what radar is and who developed it; when, why, and how it is used; and why it is important.

HOW
ENCYCLOPEDIAS
ARE ORGANIZED

Most encyclopedias are arranged alphabetically. Some have an index that tells you which articles cover a topic and lists the volumes and pages where the information appears.

General encyclopedias are a good place to start researching a topic. When you have a broad topic in mind, encyclopedias provide you with a general overview and information on the various subtopics. By examining how an encyclopedia article is organized, you can get ideas on how to narrow your topic and organize a paper. Some encyclopedias have an outline at the end of each article, which you can use as a guide when preparing a paper or report.

USING AN
ENCYCLOPEDIA

Encyclopedias list related topics and a bibliography of sources at the end of each article. If you have to do a report, the list of related topics can guide you as you decide what to write about. Once you decide on your subject, they can supply more information. The bibliography will give you a lead on sources that can provide more details.

If you don't have a topic for a report in mind, flip through the encyclopedia at random. See what catches your eye, and let that lead you to a topic you'll be interested in researching. Remember, if you are interested in the topic you're researching, you'll enjoy reading about it and finding new information. Try to avoid topics you couldn't care less about. That will make the work of preparing a report seem longer. You'll find it harder to summon the energy to do the work. If you must write about something that leaves you completely bored, motivate yourself by asking questions. "Why is this important?" "Is there anything about this topic that is interesting?" "Does any of this mean something in my life?" You never know—what you find out may surprise you!

Most libraries have several different sets of encyclopedias, including some on computer software. Before you use any encyclopedia as a source, check the copyright date. As you know, things change quickly in this world. Events in the real world may overtake information in an encyclopedia. Most encyclopedias print annual yearbooks that provide up-to-date information, however. If you're looking for details of a recent event, you might want to start by checking the yearbook.

Just as some dictionaries are specialized, so are some encyclopedias. You can find specialized encyclopedias on technology, science, wildlife, pop and rock music, sports, and space, to name just a few topics.

Atlases

When you want to know the distance from New York to San Francisco or the highest mountain in Asia, you need an atlas, which is a book of maps. Atlases are named after a character from Greek mythology. Atlas was one of a group of gods called the Titans. When Atlas and the other Titans lost a war to the gods of Mount Olympus, Atlas' punishment was to hold up the sky. Since in mythology Atlas holds up the world, his name refers to a book that holds information about the world.

WHAT CAN YOU FIND IN AN ATLAS?

Geographical atlases usually contain maps of cities, towns, roads, rivers, and mountains. They include place names and features, such as mountains. They show the size and relationships of land and water areas. An index lists features such as towns, regions, mountains, and rivers and tells you where to find them on the maps. Special maps may show information on population, climate, and plant and animal life. Some atlases include facts about different countries and cities.

But many atlases contain more than maps of countries. They also have graphs, diagrams, photos, and illustrations. Atlases give you bird's-eye views, close-ups, cross-sections, and magnifications of information. They even display maps of the ocean floor. They open up volcanoes so you can see what they look like inside. They show you how tall a mountain is by comparing its size to things you know well. You'll find ratios of land to water, desert to mountain, and rural populations to urban populations for any place you can think of, as well as some you didn't know existed.

Atlases literally bring the world to your fingertips. Several countries publish atlases showing the physical, economic, and cultural resources of their nation in great detail. You can get to know the names and geographic features of a place without ever having to go there!

GETTING UP-TO-DATE INFORMATION

Much of the information in atlases is unstable, changing from decade to decade or even year to year. Of course, the location of places doesn't change, and mountains don't disappear overnight, but populations, place names, borders, and industries change. To make sure that you are getting the most accurate, up-to-date information, check the copyright date of the atlas. You don't want to include obsolete information in a school report.

The kind of atlas that you need depends on the type of information you're seeking. If you're planning your driving route for a road trip, a road atlas will be the best one for the job. But if you're searching for information about people and cultures, you won't find a road atlas very useful. To choose an appropriate atlas, ask yourself what information you need and how in-depth it should be. Each atlas is different, and you'll find a wide variety to choose from at the library. A librarian will be delighted to help you find the atlases that will be most useful to you.

CHOOSING AN ATLAS

Almanacs

Almanacs are books or pamphlets that usually are printed yearly. Specialized almanacs contain a variety of information on one subject. General almanacs provide information on a variety of subjects. The types of information you typically can find in almanacs are noteworthy dates and events; the motion of the stars and planets; and facts and figures about governments, history, geography, and weather. You also may find population statistics, information on specific industries, and data about farming and agricultural products.

Almanacs originally were developed to give farmers and navigators information about the weather, solar and lunar eclipses, the phases of the moon, the movements of the stars, and the time of sunrise and sunset. This information helped farmers plan their crops and navigators stay on course during sea voyages.

Today, some almanacs are published by special-interest groups. For example, the almanac published by the United Nations provides facts, statistics, and documents about countries throughout the world. Other almanacs are published by newspapers, religious groups, businesses, or professions. These almanacs contain specialized information on matters important to the organization. For example, the United States Naval Observatory publishes an almanac of information for navigators and astronomers.

You can use almanacs to get information about the immediate past and the ancient past. It's fascinating to look up old volumes of the *Farmer's Almanac* or *Poor Richard's Almanac* to see what life was like in the past. If you want "just the

Encyclopedia article

Atlas

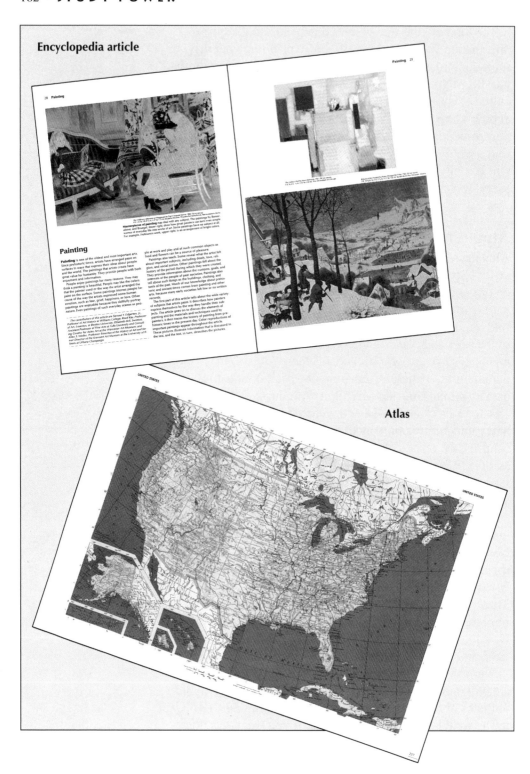

facts," an almanac is where you will find them. Which almanac you choose, of course, depends on which facts you're searching for.

Books about information

Some reference books list sources that contain the information you're looking for. *Readers' Guide to Periodical Literature* is one such source. *Readers' Guide* has been directing people to magazines and magazine articles since the early 1900's. It lists articles printed in more than 175 periodicals. There you can find the most current articles published in nontechnical magazines.

Readers' Guide is updated monthly. At the end of the year, the individual volumes are bound into one hard-cover book. So, begin your search with the most recent issue and work back. Libraries often have many years worth of *Readers' Guide* available, so you can find and locate older articles as well as the most recent. If the library subscribes to a particular magazine, the back issues will be in storage. A librarian can get you the magazine that you need. You will have access to current periodicals on the shelves. No library will have all the materials listed in *Readers' Guide*, but many libraries can borrow almost any periodical from other libraries through a service called interlibrary loan.

Entries in *Readers' Guide* are listed alphabetically by subject and author. Occasionally, articles are listed by title as well. A *Readers' Guide* entry contains the name of the magazine, date of publication, page numbers, volume and number of the periodical, and whether or not the article is illustrated. In the front of *Readers' Guide* is a key to the abbreviations used. You may need to use that key to figure out exactly what the entry means.

Readers' Guide is now available on computer. This makes searching for articles easier and faster. You simply type in your topic and the computer will supply a list of articles dealing with that topic. If it finds 10,342 articles on your topic, you can use the computer to narrow your search and make a more manageable list. The computer also will tell you whether or not your library carries that periodical and may offer an abstract of the article.

You can use many other reference sources to track down the information you're looking for. *The New York Times Index* lists and summarizes newspaper articles about national and international affairs. Entries usually are listed alphabetically by subject. The *Book Review Digest* gives you a listing and a digest, or summary, of recently published books.

Another useful source of this kind is *Books in Print*. It lists all books currently being published, not just new books. Some books have been in print for hundreds of years! If you're trying to find a book that was published in 1976, *Books in Print* will tell you whether or not it is still in print. This is good to know because if a book that you need is no longer in print, you can't order it from your local bookseller. You have to find it in a library or a used bookstore.

Books in Print organizes the information in three different ways: by title, author, and subject. Sometimes, you know only one piece of information about a book. *Books in Print* allows you to find what you're looking for when you have only incomplete information. An entry in *Books in Print* provides you with the following information: author, title, copyright date, publisher, price, whether it is in paperback or hard-cover, and more! Like *Readers' Guide*, *Books in Print* is available on computer.

Believe it or not, there's even a reference that will help you locate libraries and find out about their collections. The *American Library Directory* helps you locate approximately 20,000 libraries in the United States.

Most of the time, your community or school library will probably suit your needs. But libraries specializing in law,

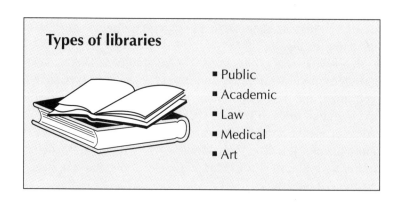

Types of libraries

- Public
- Academic
- Law
- Medical
- Art

medicine, art, religion, and other topics also exist. If you need to, you can find out which library has the best collection of books on the subject you're focusing on. Such a library would be a great place to do your research.

Judging sources

Once you begin gathering information, you must decide whether a particular source is useful or not. Even a highly reliable source may not suit your purposes. To decide if a source is one that will help you, first you must ask yourself the following questions.

What is the scope of coverage? Scan the index to see how many pages of the book are devoted to your topic. If your topic is not listed, think of other headings that your topic may be under. Look under those headings. If only a few pages deal with your topic, skim those pages to see whether the information is something you might need. If many pages are devoted to your topic, put the book aside—you'll probably want to use it. Be careful, though. Too much information can be almost as useless as too little information. Keep your eyes open for a source that presents what you're looking for in a way that you can understand easily. You probably won't have time to read entire books on a subject.

SCOPE OF COVERAGE

When was the book published? If the topic you are researching is in a rapidly changing field—such as science, medicine, or technology—you should use the most recently published sources. If your topic is more stable, such as the events of the Industrial Revolution, copyright dates don't matter as much. In fact, you may want to get a book that was published during the era you are researching. That will give you a firsthand account of the event. The copyright usually appears in the front of the book on the back of the title page.

PUBLICATION DATE

Is the author an authority on the subject? Some authorities are well-known, such as James McPherson on the Civil War, Carl Sandburg on Abraham Lincoln, and Carl Sagan on physics. Because these individuals' reputations precede them, you know that their works are recognized for validity.

AUTHORITATIVE AUTHOR

Examples of reference books by topic

Bibliographies and catalogs
Software Reviews on File; Directories in Print; Book Review Digest

Psychology
Dictionary of Behavioral Science; Encyclopedia of Psychology; The Family Mental Health Encyclopedia

Law
Martindale-Hubbel Law Directory®; Encyclopedia of the American Constitution; Legal Resource Directory

Business
Moody's Bond Record; The Sourcebook of Zip Code Demographics; Ward's Business Directory of Public and Private Companies; Brands and Their Companies

Science
Today's Science on File; The New Book of Popular Science; Science Fair Project Index

Mathematics
Handbook of Mathematical Functions; Handbook of Mathematical Tables and Formulas

Medicine
Dictionary of Medical Specialities; The Essential Guide to Prescription Drugs; The Johns Hopkins Medical Handbook

The arts
The Oxford Companion to Twentieth Century Art; Historic Architecture Sourcebook; Dictionary of American Painters, Sculptors, and Engravers

College and careers
Barron's Profile of American Colleges; Peterson's Register of Higher Education; The Almanac of International Jobs and Careers

Literature
Dictionary of Mythology, Folklore, and Symbols; Oxford Dictionary of Proverbs; The Cambridge Encyclopedia of Language

Geography and history
The Columbia History of the World; Dictionary of the History of Ideas; Who Was Who in World Exploration

Biography
The McGraw Hill Encyclopedia of World Biography

Other authors are less well-known, but just as authoritative. If you are curious about the author's authority on a subject, read the blurb about him or her on the back of the book or the flap of the dust jacket. Check the author in a biographical dictionary or encyclopedia. Look up the author's name in *Books in Print* to see how many books the author has written and who published them. If you are unfamiliar with the publisher, ask the librarian about how carefully that publisher checks its facts. Many publishers' reputations have been built or ruined based on whether or not they publish accurate information.

Another way to get an idea of the author's authority on a subject is to look for the author's reference sources. You'll find that information in footnotes, appendixes, and bibliographies. These are signs that the writer's research was thorough.

Is the author biased? You want your source to be objective. If the author gives only one side of an argument, you also will be reporting only one side of an issue. On emotional topics such as wars, the environment, and religion, it's important to find out who the opposing sides are and what they believe. Draw your information from more than one side.

AUTHOR BIAS

Which edition of the book are you looking at? If more than one edition of a book was printed, you should have the latest edition. This most recent edition will contain corrections to any mistakes made in previous editions. A book that has several editions indicates that the book is popular and respected, and therefore you can probably assume that it is authoritative.

BOOK EDITIONS

For whom is this book intended? Some books are written for other authorities in the field. If a source you have located is such a book, the information may be over your head. Look for books that are written so that people with little or no prior knowledge on a subject can learn about it.

A BOOK'S AUDIENCE

What special features does the book have? Special features such as charts, maps, tables, graphs, illustrations, bibliographies, chapter summaries, or chapter outlines will help you use a book. If there are lots of graphics, you can include some of them in your report. If you do so, be sure to indicate where you got the graphic.

A BOOK'S SPECIAL FEATURES

As you begin to use reference books, you may be startled to find that the facts in one book or article disagree with the facts in another. Even basic facts, such as the area of a country, may be different in an encyclopedia and an almanac. Or a recent finding reported in a magazine article may conflict with information in a medical encyclopedia. When you run up against this problem, consult a third source that usually contains reliable, up-to-date information. Ask a librarian to recommend a source if you're not sure which to use. If the information in the third source agrees with either the first or second, that should resolve the dispute.

If you're planning to use in your report data that you've been unable to verify, be sure to identify where the information comes from. You may say, "According to the X encyclopedia, elephants may grow to be 10 feet tall." Or state the information as a range, "Elephants may grow to be between 10 and 13 feet tall."

The public library

"You don't need to know very much to start with, if you know the way to the public library."

Lesley Conger

Now that you know what references and resources are available, it's time to take an armchair tour of the library, because no other single location is going to bring you such a wide range of sources.

The word *library* comes from the Latin word *liber*, which means *book*. But a library's collection consists of much more than books! Libraries hold ideas, historical accounts, stories, recipes, jokes, how-to tips, and more—in the form of books, newspapers, magazines, videotapes, audiotapes, computer software, microfiche, microfilm, periodicals, art prints, musical scores, and maps.

Whatever your likes and dislikes, the library has something for you. Libraries strive to offer many kinds of materials to serve the special needs of their patrons. For example, libraries have large-print or braille books for those who are partially sighted or blind. At different points in your life, you use the library for different reasons. A library may offer story time for

young children and book-discussion groups for adults. As your needs change, the library is responsible for seeing that you get whatever information you need, in whatever form you need it. Whether you want to know what state a company is based in, how to fix a faucet, or the history of jam, you can find that answer at the library.

Libraries bring you in touch with the ideas, knowledge, and experience of other people, countries, and centuries. Near or far, new or old, humorous or serious, real or make-believe, poetry or prose—it's all housed in the library, waiting for you to check it out. Almost everyone has read library books for one reason or another. Students use libraries to find out more about a subject they are studying in school. People of all ages use libraries to get magazines, videos, tapes, and the latest book by their favorite author. Those with special hobbies use the library to learn more about them. Browsers come in hoping to find something that suits their mood. People of any age, from 3 to 93, are catered to at the library.

PROVIDING
MATERIALS

ASSISTING PATRONS

Librarians do more than buy books, catalog them, and put them on shelves. Librarians can find the answer to almost any question. They can show you how to use the library and the materials it holds.

Feel free to call the library to ask whether a book or video is available. If the materials you ask for are not checked out by another patron, the librarian will have them waiting for you when you get there. If you need a book that your library doesn't own, your librarian can track it down through the interlibrary loan system. If it is at a nearby public library, it will be held for you there until you can pick it up. Otherwise, it will be sent to your local library, usually within a couple of weeks at most.

Libraries provide reference and information services. Many libraries have a number you can call to use this service. You can call to ask a question such as, "Who composed the Australian national anthem?" Some libraries help patrons with job searches. Patrons considering certain investments can get financial information at the public library.

In addition, many libraries keep their reference and information lines open after hours. So, if you're up late working on a report and you need to verify the date of the Sepoy Rebellion, chances are you can call the library.

COMMUNITY SERVICE

Libraries strive to serve people in the community by providing whatever type of information they need. But libraries do a lot more than distribute information and help you to find exactly what you're looking for. Libraries assist groups as well as individuals. If you are a member of a club or committee, librarians will help you prepare community service programs. They schedule presentations and organize events as well. Libraries post their schedule of events and have copies for you to take home. Which of these types of programs does your public library sponsor: story hours? discussion groups? lectures? films? music recitals?

Did you know that you don't always have to go to the library? Sometimes the library comes to you. Look for the bookmobile in your neighborhood. Librarians make every effort to get materials to people who can't get to the library. Many libraries deliver materials to people in hospitals, prisons, and remote areas.

You probably know where to find the books, tapes, and videos in your local library, but it may be more difficult for you to find your way around the reference room. The reference area of your library is a fascinating place for people who know their way around it, but it can be daunting for those who don't. If you feel a little intimidated, ask a librarian to explain how the reference area is organized.

THE REFERENCE ROOM

The vertical file is where the pamphlets, newspaper or magazine clippings, pictures, and other materials that are fragile or difficult to shelve are stored. A vertical file is like a catch-all drawer, a place to store things that you need but don't know where to put. However, in a vertical file, the articles are organized into file folders that are labeled by subject. You will be able to locate information on topics such as the environment, current issues, health, and government services. Some libraries allow you to check out individual files.

THE VERTICAL FILE

PERIODICALS

When you're researching the status of women in Sweden or the progress of land reform in El Salvador, you need more than the usual fare to choose from. You're sure to find all the local daily newspapers at your library. But did you know that you can also find newspapers from other parts of the country and foreign papers as well? Daily newspapers not only keep you abreast of current events, they report the emotional impact of a particular event.

Editorials and letters to the editor give you firsthand reactions to the news of the day. In different parts of the country and in other nations, the news may be reported with a different emphasis. If you are researching a topic, you'll want to see how an event is being perceived outside your hometown. You can also find back issues of major newspapers in your library either on microfilm or in print—ask your librarian what form your library uses.

Magazines and journals report on different topics. Some specialize in current events. Literary journals publish poems, short stories, and novel extracts. You'll find magazines that focus on a particular hobby. Others report developments that affect a particular profession.

Periodicals also vary in how they present information. Many mainstream periodicals present information in a highly visual way, using not only photographs but maps, graphs, charts, tables, diagrams, drawings, and cartoons. Some popular periodicals are not respected sources of information and so will not be available at your library. However, your library will stock more obscure periodicals that are respected but not readily available through newsstands, such as publications for specialists in a particular field.

Some of the magazines that you get at home, from the grocery store, or at newsstands will have articles that you need. But can you guarantee that you've kept the issue from three years ago or even a month ago? A library can. The library will either have the periodicals listed in *Readers' Guide* or it will be able to get them for you. That's service!

AUDIO-VISUAL
RESOURCES

Do you need a compact disc, a video, or an audiotape? What about a filmstrip, phonograph record, or microfiche edition of a book that is too rare for your library to buy? Many libraries have extensive collections of multimedia materials.

What a luxury! You can learn a foreign language, listen to Ella Fitzgerald's first recording, or read an out-of-print book from the 1700's all in the same place. Libraries let you use the most modern, up-to-date equipment to go back in time. It's great to have so much available for your amusement or education.

Although libraries don't supply career counseling, they do house information on careers, business trends, résumé writing, and job hunting. You'll also find catalogs describing colleges throughout the country, the scholarships they offer, and college entrance examinations. When you're searching for a college or career that will suit you, the library may be a good place to start.

CAREER, COLLEGE GUIDANCE

Many people use maps mostly to find the locations of places and roads. While maps help your family plan trips, you also can use them to follow news events in different parts of the world. Maps can make these faraway places and events seem more real to you.

MAPS AND GLOBES

Globes can give you an accurate picture of the earth as a whole. You can observe distances, areas, and directions on a globe without the distortion of flat maps. A globe shows the positions of land and oceans as they are on earth. You can also get globes of the moon, planets, and constellations.

Make sure that any map or globe you use is a recent one. That way, you'll know it reflects political changes, such as in the names and boundaries of countries, throughout the world.

The best way to learn about your library is to go there. You'll find out what computer databases (computerized indexes) you can use to get information. With the speed and amount of data that a computer gives you, you won't have any trouble figuring what sources to use. Most likely, you'll be trying to figure out which ones to ignore, so that you aren't researching information from hundreds of different sources.

VISIT YOUR LIBRARY

Remember, if you need help using a resource or finding information, ask a librarian. Librarians have been specially trained to know exactly where to find information and how to use the available resources. They will welcome your questions. Part of being at ease in a library is knowing how to use the services it offers.

Other resources

In addition to the more "traditional" reference sources, you can use many other ways to find information—and learn more about the world around you. Some of these resources are described in the following section.

COMPUTERS

Computers are fast becoming the resource of choice. With improved technology and advanced software, computers put a wealth of information at your fingertips, and quickly.

You may not have a computer at home, but you don't have to own one to use one. Many libraries, schools, and community centers offer computers for public use.

Computers put you in touch with large amounts of information by means of "on-line services." Over phone lines with the use of a modem, you can connect with other computers all over the world. On-line services work with databases. Database searches save you time by doing in minutes what used to take days.

These searches provide you with a list of materials that contain the information you need. Computerized indexes often offer more than printed indexes. Often, they are more up-to-date. The computer can search them for terms and information sources too current to appear in printed indexes. You can use computer searches to combine related aspects of a topic, such as steroids and athletes, to produce a list of materials that is tailored specifically to your topic.

Among the variety of subjects that you can study with the aid of computers are spelling, vocabulary, math, biology, history, foreign languages, and numerous other subjects. With computer-aided instruction (CAI), the computer takes you through a lesson step-by-step. Most CAI software even has a built-in evaluation system to grade your performance. Perhaps the most useful aspect of CAI is that you can learn at your own pace.

LEARNING THROUGH THE MEDIA

The traditional idea of "learning" is that of a student bent over a desk, listening to every word a teacher says. But, as you know, you learn from all kinds of people and in all kinds of places. If your hobby is baseball, for example, how did you learn most about it—by reading a book, taking a class, or watching television?

Much of what is on television, radio, and video exists to entertain, but it also informs. Depending on how you use these media, they can add to your education.

Not all television shows are pure entertainment. A wide variety of shows teach as well. Almost any kind of information you can imagine can come into your home through the television screen.

Some shows are designed primarily to educate, and these also entertain to different degrees. High school and college-level courses that are broadcast on television fall into this category. They provide enough entertainment to keep you tuned in, but their main purpose is to teach. But what about the nature, geography, history, science, and health-care shows that present information in such an appealing way that you are fascinated by what you are seeing and hearing? Shows that are both educational and entertaining can open up whole worlds to you.

Watching television is worthwhile if you choose shows that stretch your imagination and give you pleasure. Remember, in Chapter 2 we said that learning often begins with an attraction. You pay attention to what interests you. If what interests you happens to be a television show, it presents no less of an opportunity to learn than a book does. To make the most out of the time you spend watching television, take a moment or two each week to flip through the television guide to see whether it lists any shows on a topic you are studying or interested in.

You have two choices when you watch educational shows. You can simply sit back and enjoy them, or you can be an active viewer. If you are using the show as learning tool, be active by deciding what to watch. Then, before the show begins, think about what you already know on the topic and make a list of questions you hope the program will answer. If you have the time, do some background reading. Be active while you watch by asking yourself questions or taking notes. Be active afterward as well. Find answers to your lingering questions by talking to others or reading about the topic.

If you find a particular program especially illuminating, try to get a transcript of it. The producers or sponsors of many special programs prepare transcripts, bibliographies, and sup-plementary materials for viewers upon request.

Videos are another way to use television as a learning tool. You can find videotapes on just about any subject. The best source of information about videotapes is the *Video Source Book*. You can find it in the reference area of most libraries.

RADIO

Radio talk shows give you an opportunity to hear different points of view about a variety of subjects, such as the arts, local and national government, and health. Some programs encourage you to call in with your views or questions. News programs keep you on top of current events. Many daily newspapers publish a schedule of radio programs. Look at the radio guide to see if there are any programs that you'd like to make the time to listen to.

One of the benefits of audiotapes is their portability. Having a tape means being able to listen to anything as many times as you wish, anytime you wish. With the availability of car stereos, portable tape players, and headphones, you can listen to tapes as you commute, exercise, or run errands. It's just as easy to listen to a tape on the move as it is to listen at home. You can buy tapes prerecorded or make your own.

AUDIOTAPES

Types of tapes

Prerecorded	**Homemade tapes**
Books	Self-improvement
Transcripts of radio or television shows	Lectures
	Classes
Music	A selection of your favorite songs
Foreign language instruction	A spoken "letter" to a friend
Motivational	

All around you are people who are willing and able to help you. Many family members, friends, co-workers, librarians, teachers, or classmates will gladly help you in whatever way they can.

HUMAN RESOURCES

If the people you know can't give you the type of information you need, seek out professionals in the field you are studying. You will find that people such as health-care professionals and business people usually are more than willing to share their expertise. Also, many volunteer organizations offer information. The *Directory of Associations* lists hundreds of organizations, their addresses and phone numbers, and names of people to contact. Whatever you're looking for, there is bound to be a person willing to talk to you.

Don't overlook people who have experienced an event first- or secondhand. Talking with someone who actually lived through World War II is likely to be more interesting than reading about it in books. You may conduct an interview or let the other person tell you stories—whichever way you find most comfortable.

Textbooks exist specifically to teach you about a particular subject. As you probably already know, however, some do a better job than others. Some textbooks make a dry topic lively and exciting. Others make the most interesting topic seem deathly dull.

Here are some recognized signs of a well-written textbook:

1. It helps you select important information. Headings and subheadings convey main ideas. Introductions and summaries highlight important aspects of the subject. Questions or objectives focus readers' attention on key points. Main ideas are obvious.

2. It helps readers organize important information. Headings and subheadings reflect a reasonable organization of the subject matter. The structure is clearly signaled throughout the text. Connections are explicit or obvious. References are clear. Transition statements help the reader move from idea to idea. The order of events in the text is logical and easy to follow. Tables and charts organize critical information.

3. It helps readers pull together important elements. Questions or activities help students relate what they have read to what they already know.

4. It contains accurate, consistent information.

HOW ABOUT YOUR TEXTBOOKS?

Now that you know the signs of a well-written textbook, it will be interesting for you to take a look at some of your own textbooks. Your answers will help you see why you learn more easily from some books than others. Examining your own textbooks will also help you see how you can get information from them most efficiently.

Answer each question using the following scale:

Excellent—This book is extremely useful
Good—This book is useful
Acceptable—This book is somewhat useful
Fair—This book is not very useful
Poor—This book is not at all useful

1. Emphasis
   a. Are the main ideas clearly stated?
   b. Do subheadings accurately reflect the content that follows them?
   c. Are main ideas for the chapter stated clearly at the beginning of the chapter and repeated at the end?
   d. Are important ideas stated in positive, not negative, terms?
   e. Does the author give the main ideas the most attention?
   f. Are subtopics defined or explained and examples given?

2. Unity
   a. Are all the ideas presented related to the main ideas and major points?
   b. Does the text avoid trivial information and stick to the subject?
   c. Can the paragraphs be outlined easily?
   d. Is it easy to see relationships between ideas and follow the information presented?

3. Coherence
   a. Do the paragraphs flow naturally from one to the next?
   b. Do the pronouns have clear references to the nouns that they replace?
   c. Are concepts and relationships stated clearly? Can you identify cause and effect? Are comparisons and contrasts easy to pick out? Can you see why or how the information fits together?

4. Appropriate repetition
   a. Are all new concepts related to those that were introduced previously?
   b. Are new concepts restated to reinforce your understanding?
   c. Are references to other parts of the book given so you can easily locate more information on the topic?
   d. Are the subtopics discussed in relation to one another and related to the main topic?
   e. Are important ideas reinforced by repetition and explanations about how they relate to new information?

5. Clarity
   a. Has the author provided clear and concise examples?
   b. Are abstract ideas made concrete by giving examples?
   c. Is it easy to see how examples relate to what they clarify?

6. Appropriate vocabulary
   a. Are new ideas introduced in familiar terms?
   b. Are technical terms introduced gradually and defined with familiar words, boldfaced, or highlighted?
   c. Are concepts developed in terms that are understood, and if not, are the new terms defined?
   d. Does the text give clear, concrete, precise definitions?

7. Appropriate reading level
   a. Does the text relate new information to experiences that you can understand and respond to?
   b. Is the vocabulary and language intended to speak to you or someone older or younger?
   c. Does the author let you know what information you are expected to be familiar with and what information is expected to be new to you?

8. Format
   a. Is the book attractive?
   b. Are the graphic aids useful?
   c. Are ideas or concepts highlighted by use of italicized type, boldface headings, and spacing of words on a page?
   d. Do the questions asked, if any, help you think more clearly about the ideas presented?
   e. Does the text help you find information by providing an index, a glossary, chapter summaries, and so on?

Information is everywhere

You may have found that some of your textbooks are not as much of a help as you'd like them to be. Now that you've finished this chapter, you should have a good idea of how you can supplement the information in your textbooks through alternative sources. If your history textbook's account of World War I is nothing but a tedious list of battles and dates, for example, you may try searching out a more lively book on the same subject. Or why not read some of the stories of people who lived through the war—people who fought in the trenches, worked in munitions factories, or fled the war as refugees? Firsthand accounts, where people describe their experiences and emotions, can make historical events seem real to you, and relevant to your own life.

It's truly amazing how many books there are, how many subjects have been written about, how many stories and poems have been created—and how different they can be from one another. With so many resources available to you in school, at your local library, and through computers and television, it's sometimes hard not to be overwhelmed! Some people even have a name for this feeling—it's called "information overload."

INFORMATION OVERLOAD

By following the steps outlined in this chapter, you should be able to find your way through a wide variety of reference sources without becoming confused. You may have so much fun searching for information that you'll want to do more.

Books are indeed resources for learning, but more than that, they are passports and companions. When you read a book, you can visit places that really exist and those that don't. There are even books about places that once existed, but have now disappeared in the mists of time. You can get to know people who are long dead. You can laugh at the antics of fictitious characters, and come to think of them as friends. A world of fascinating people, places, and things is waiting for you now to discover.

BOOKS SHOW YOU THE WORLD

Books will educate you, enrich you, and entertain you. So don't limit yourself to reading only assigned works or works for reference. Make sure that every day you are reading for pleasure, too!

"WORRY
IS
A
WASTE
OF
ENERGY."

KATHERINE
MANSFIELD

CHAPTER

5

WHERE TO
TURN FOR
HELP

✎ Tackling problems

✎ Steps toward solutions

✎ Open up

When you're confronting one of the problems that face every student at one time or another, you may feel at a loss. It may seem as though one problem leads to another, which in turn spawns others. Brad, for example, is falling behind in math. So, he decides to work really hard to catch up. He's spending so much of his time on math that he starts falling behind with his English assignments. He needs to take a second look at his study plan now, before things get worse.

No matter whether the problem is personal or academic, you can do many things to make it less ominous. Often, you can solve it completely. Left unattended, however, personal problems can lead to academic problems and academic problems can lead to personal problems.

Tackling problems

Imagine, for example, that you recently started a part-time job. You like the work, but three nights a week you are simply too exhausted to do your homework. Meanwhile, the assignments keep piling up. You may feel panicky or angry or scared. Or, you may become discouraged and wonder, "What is the point of even trying?"

Before you begin madly rushing to finish assignments, STOP. Simply do nothing until you make a plan. If you scramble to finish your work, you may make careless errors in your haste. Your grades may start slipping. Suppose you stay up late every night to complete your assignments. But you're too tired to study well at night and too tired to concentrate at school and too tired to be patient with customers at work, and too tired to do anything but snap at your parents when they mention the situation. The problem is snowballing. But you still have time to do something about it.

In fact, it's never too late to face a problem. You may need to get advice or help from others, or you may be able to handle it on your own. But you have to do something—and the sooner, the better.

TAKE ACTION

Problems are like spills; they have to be cleaned up. Some spills are easier to handle than others. Water will dry off even if you don't mop it up. But try leaving milk where it splatters: It stains and goes sour and smells bad. If that happens, the stain is not the first thing others notice, the rancid odor is. And that odor is more difficult to cover up than the stain.

When you have a problem, the "stain" may be a low grade, a break-up with your boyfriend or girlfriend, or a dent in the fender. The "stink" may come as a black mood, depression, anger, or withdrawal into your own little world.

Problems have consequences. At first, the consequences are small, but as problems grow, you may begin to doubt yourself. When that happens, you lose some of your confidence and self-esteem, which in turn feeds more negative thinking.

To stop this cycle, you need to step back from your problems. That will give you the perspective you need to figure out what to do. Often, people are harder on themselves than they would be on a friend in the same situation. One way to get perspective on a problem is to pretend it isn't yours. Imagine your best friend had this problem. How would you treat him or her? Treat yourself the same way.

PUT IT IN PERSPECTIVE

For example, suppose you're still struggling with trying to do your school assignments while holding down your part-time job. You're tired and scared. You keep telling yourself that other students can handle this situation, so you have no excuse for not doing so. Ask yourself, "What would I say to a friend? Would I say it was all her own fault? Or would I offer some practical suggestions?"

Looking at the problem from a distance may help you see some solutions. Maybe you'll decide to get up early to study instead of trying to do it after work. Maybe you'll decide to work only on weekends. Maybe you'll decide to do homework from 4 to 6 p.m. and work from 7 to 9 p.m., instead of the other way around. Whatever you decide, stepping back from a problem will help you see that it's not insolvable and you are not an idiot for having it.

Another way to put things in perspective is to ask yourself, "What's the worst thing that could happen?" Have you hurt a friend? What's the worst thing that could happen? You could lose a friend. On the other hand, you could talk to your friend or write a letter saying sorry or explaining your feelings. A stronger friendship could result. Have you cheated on a test? What's the worst thing that could happen? You could get suspended. Yet, you could talk to your teacher. Your teacher may suggest that you write a report on the assignment so that you have a chance to learn the information for yourself and show what you understand. Your teacher may even admire your courage in facing the situation. Have you lied to your parents? What's the worst thing that could happen? If they heard the truth from someone else, you would have to work hard to win back their trust. If you told them yourself, they would be angry at first. But in the long run, their respect for and trust in you would grow. Together, you could agree about what to do if a similar situation came up in the future.

Your attitude affects your ability to solve a problem. If you can think only about how awful everything is, that will make you more likely to ignore or hide from the problem. But, if you look for the good that may come out of the situation, you will find the courage to face the problem.

Steps toward solutions

The first step toward solving a problem is to recognize that the problem exists. The second step is simply to stop. Stop ignoring the problem. Stop kicking yourself for having a problem. Stop blaming yourself for the problem. Once you get some perspective and calm down, you can start working on a plan. The third step is to break down your plan—and the problem—into smaller parts. The fourth step is to implement your plan.

Rebecca, for example, cannot seem to work at a steady pace. She invariably waits until the night before an assignment is due to start working on it. Then, she works late into the night, getting only three hours' sleep. She feels exhausted the next day, and she never gets the grade she knows she could earn if she worked less frantically. Because she feels so terrible every time she completes assignments, she dreads working on them. That's why she can't get down to work until her back is against the wall.

What can Rebecca do about this vicious circle? Once she recognizes that she avoids assignments because she links them with worry and exhaustion, she can try to change that. That's a big order because she's been acting and thinking this way for years. So, she decides to try spending half an hour every day on a particular assignment, a history essay. Every time she does so, she rewards herself in some way. She watches a favorite TV show, takes a bubble bath, or eats a favorite treat. Instead of blaming herself for her old way of thinking, she's taking small steps to change it. And, by rewarding herself, she's giving herself lots of reasons to change.

CHOOSE YOUR REACTION

Believe it or not, you can decide how to react to a problem. Give yourself time to decide what reaction would be best. It may seem as though you have no time to think, but unless you take the time anyway, you may make things worse.

Think about a fast-moving basketball game. The stronger team makes the opponents run up and down the court, wearing themselves out. Finally, one exhausted player gets the ball and takes control by slowing down the action. This gives the team members time to plan their next moves. Slow the game down when you need to, so you have more time to think.

RELAX

As odd as it may sound, and as tense as you may feel, you must relax before you can find good solutions to problems. When you're tense, you're closed to options. You tend to act impulsively and you inadvertently may make matters worse. If you can relax, however, you give yourself a chance to see the big picture.

PSYCH YOURSELF UP

If you're struggling with work, school, friends, family, or all four, you probably feel at a pretty low ebb. You must psych yourself up—reaffirm your belief in yourself. Do something that makes you feel good. Solving a problem is going to take energy and commitment, so you need to put yourself in the right frame of mind.

Some people benefit from reciting affirmations. Affirmations are statements that focus on your strengths. Always say affirmations in the present tense, to reinforce that this is the way things are now.

Try repeating an affirmation several times immediately after you wake up or just before you go to sleep each day. Or, try saying one when you catch yourself blaming yourself for something that goes wrong. Instead of saying, "Why did I do that? I can't believe I'm so stupid!" try saying, "I've handled problems before, I can handle this now."

Here are some examples of affirmations:
"I can handle whatever comes my way."

"I am capable of handling this problem."

"I am smart enough to solve this problem."

"I have enough time in my day to accomplish all the things I need to."

"I have the support of my family, friends, and teachers."

VISUALIZATION

Visualization is another way of helping you mentally prepare to solve problems. Picture yourself solving the problem, step by step. Picture yourself at the end of the road, having solved the problem and feeling good about it.

For example, if you're completely lost in calculus class, imagine talking to your teacher about it. Imagine how good it would feel if everything became clear. Picture yourself finishing your calculus homework in 20 minutes instead of three hours. Imagine yourself holding a test paper in your hand, with your name at the top, along with the highest grade you can hope for. Hold onto that image and the feeling that goes along with it as you take the first step and talk to your teacher.

WHAT CAN YOU CONTROL?

When you feel ready to take steps toward solving a problem, focus on the aspects that you can control. For example, if you are late handing in an assignment, don't focus on the date it was due. You can do nothing about that now. Instead, pick a new due date to work toward. If a friend is angry with you, don't focus on what you did wrong. Your friend is already angry, so now you need to come together to make peace.

Think about what you can do, not what you can't undo.

Your plan might have to include several short-term goals that let you achieve your long-term goal. For example, if you are behind in several classes, or missed several assignments in one class, you need to catch up one assignment at a time. If you tried to do everything all at once, you would defeat yourself before you began. Set up a timetable that will let you keep up with your present assignments while doing some catch-up work. Make it possible for you to succeed.

Also, acknowledge that there are some problems that you can't control. Suppose your parents are getting divorced. Given the turmoil at home, you find it hard to concentrate at school. That's completely natural. No one can completely switch off personal problems. What can you do about this situation? Acknowledge that your parents' decision to divorce is beyond your control. Ask yourself what you can do to make the situation better for yourself. Perhaps it would help to study in the peace and quiet of the library. Perhaps you'd feel better if you confided in a friend whose parents are divorced. Perhaps you think your teachers should know why you've been unprepared in class these days. Although the larger problem—your parents' divorce—is beyond your control, you can take steps to lessen its impact on you.

Open up

It's a sign of maturity to say to someone, "I know that I'm having a problem. I'm having trouble figuring out how to solve it. Can you help me make a plan?" Family, friends, and teachers may be waiting for you to ask for their help.

If you fail to let others know that you are working on the problem, they may misinterpret your actions. They may think

that you don't see the problem, or don't care. If you start getting those signals from the people around you, you may start fighting them instead of the problem. If you are wary of talking to your parents or teachers, try talking to siblings, friends, or friends' parents first. That can give you the confidence to talk to your own parents or teachers.

Sometimes, a problem is very personal. Perhaps you'd rather not discuss it with family, or even with close friends. In times like this, it may help to speak to a member of the clergy or a professional therapist. Oddly enough, it's often easier to discuss personal matters with a stranger than with someone you see every day.

You may feel as if you're the only one who knows what you're going through. But if you reach out to others, you'll begin to feel less isolated, awkward, or ashamed. If you ask how others dealt with similar problems, you'll learn about pitfalls to avoid and solutions to try.

CHOOSING A
CONFIDANT

Think carefully before you decide to confide in someone. Talk to someone with whom you are completely comfortable. Choose someone who lets you be yourself and will listen to what you say, even if it sounds silly or unreasonable.

If you're uncomfortable talking to someone, you probably

don't feel safe enough to be completely honest. Your discomfort may be a signal that you don't trust this person. Or, it may stem from shame or guilt on your part. If this is the case, let your confidant know exactly how you're feeling. Perhaps he or she will be able to put you at ease.

It may help to talk to more than one person. If you get different opinions about what to do, you can weigh each piece of advice and choose the solution that best suits you.

WHAT TO SAY

If you want to confide in someone but can't find the words, you can start by saying that. Simply say, "I'd like to talk with you, but I don't know where to begin." Or try saying, "I'd like to talk with you, can we take a walk?" Or, "I'd like to talk with you, but I have a hard time knowing when it's a good time for you."

If you have something that is really difficult to discuss, do so when you don't have to make eye contact. It's often difficult to look at someone when you're talking about personal matters. So, talk in the car or over the phone if that's easier.

Try to focus on your own feelings without attacking or accusing the other person. For example, suppose Emma's sister agreed to go shopping with her but didn't show up. If Emma says, "Where on earth were you? This is the most selfish thing you've ever done. You never think of anyone but yourself!" her sister probably will become very defensive. Instead of discussing this incident, she's likely to start listing times when she put others first, or times when Emma was selfish. Instead, Emma says, "I'm really mad at you because you didn't show up. I was scared something happened to you. It hurts that our plans didn't really matter to you." That way, she's focusing on how she feels—something that her sister cannot deny or contradict.

Try to stick to your point and persist until you have gotten it across. Don't let the other person deflect your attention by dragging up old arguments. For example, suppose Emma's sister responds with, "That's ridiculous! You're so touchy! Everyone says so!" Emma may fall into the trap and ask, "Oh yeah? Who says so?" Before she knows it, they're talking about whether Emma is too touchy, not whether her sister was in the wrong. But Emma can avoid the trap and simply say, "Nevertheless, that's how I feel."

It's often difficult to discuss a problem. It's hard to make the first move. But it's easier to keep the door open once you open it in the first place.

TALKING TO FAMILY MEMBERS

Your parents, siblings, grandparents, aunts, uncles, and cousins all have something in common with you. All of you are part of the same family. Everyone knows everyone else. So if you're having a problem with one member of your family, talking to someone who knows and understands you both can be a good place to start.

If you are not yet ready to approach your father about something, practicing on another family member can be a big help. For example, if you have your brother listen to you, he may point out statements you need to reword, where you could be more clear, and so on. Your brother can even pretend to be your father and ask questions he's likely to ask.

By rehearsing before you discuss a problem with a parent, you give yourself a better chance of saying exactly what you mean. You also can do it the other way around—rehearse with parents when you need to talk with your siblings. For example, suppose your brother always takes your bike without asking and leaves it on the driveway when he's finished. You've done everything you can think of to make him stop, from taking his things to screaming. A parent may be able to suggest a new approach.

Also, remember that sometimes families are not ready to hear what you want to tell them. They may have their own reasons for preferring to close their ears. For example, maybe Art doesn't like the way his dad acts when he brings a girl home. Art thinks his dad flirts with Art's female friends, and he doesn't like it one bit. If Art mentions this to his mother, she may be very sympathetic and agree to speak to his dad about it. On the other hand, she may tell him to stop imagining things. When something is bothering you and you can't get help within the family, don't ignore your feelings. Look for somebody outside the family who will listen to you.

TALKING TO TEACHERS

Your teachers can help you work out problems. Some teachers may offer help, others may need to be asked. When you seek help, they can offer suggestions and guidance. Arrange a conference with your teacher at a time that's convenient for both of you, so that you both can come prepared.

If you are discussing an academic problem, have your books, notes, assignments, and questions on hand. Be prepared to say what you've done to figure out the problem on your own. You'll get more help that way because it's likely that your approach is part of the problem. A teacher often can see that when you cannot. Approach the conference willing to discuss ideas. Be open with your teacher and receptive to what he or she says.

If your academic problems stem from personal problems, discuss the situation with a teacher you trust and respect. If you reach out to your teacher, chances are that your teacher will reach back. People who choose teaching as a profession often do so because they like people and want to help. Remember, you need to be fair to yourself. If you're finding it hard to concentrate at school because of tension at home, your teacher should know that.

The good thing about discussing a personal problem with a teacher is that he or she is not personally involved. So, your teacher can see the problem from an outsider's perspective. You'll find it reassuring, calming, and worthwhile to talk with someone who can listen with an open mind, and perhaps suggest a new approach to the situation.

Another person at school to talk with about personal problems is a guidance counselor. Counselors are trained to help you with personal problems. They are required to keep everything you say to them confidential as long as it doesn't endanger your life. If you are reluctant to see a counselor, ask yourself what is the worst thing that could happen if you did. Then, ask yourself what's the worst thing that could happen if you didn't see a counselor. If that doesn't help make up your mind, make a list of pros and cons. Getting yourself help when you need it is a sign of strength and conviction.

A GUIDANCE COUNSELOR

Counselors are often a good choice for discussing family problems. Because they are trained in family issues, they often can tell you that your problem is not unique. For example, Rafael is the oldest child in his family. Now that he is a teenager, he wants to spend more free time with his friends and less with his family. When he is at home, he prefers to be alone in his room. Rafael's parents and siblings are very hurt by this behavior. They think Rafael is rejecting them. This has led to many fights. A counselor would be able to assure Rafael that most families have these fights as children become adolescents. Needing more privacy and preferring peers to family are a normal part of adolescence. Because Rafael is the oldest child, however, his family has not yet learned this.

If you are struggling with a personal problem, a counselor may be able to suggest a support group that could help. A support group is made up of people who are dealing with similar issues. Some support groups, for example, exist to help the children of alcoholics. Support groups are made up of people who have had similar experiences. Because of that, support groups can offer good advice on how to tackle certain problems. And it's a relief to know that there are others who share your problems.

TUTORS

If you are having trouble keeping up in class, you may want to consider hiring a tutor. When choosing a tutor, interview several and pick the one whose personality and philosophy most appeal to you. Take the time to get to know your tutor. It may feel awkward at first to discuss your schoolwork with

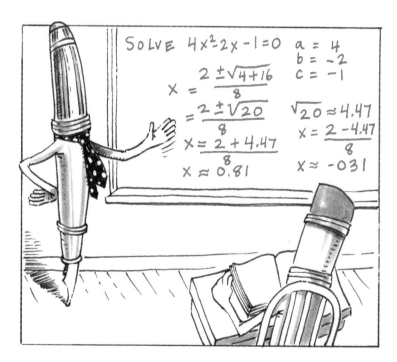

someone who is practically a stranger, but it will get easier.

Sometimes, group tutoring is more effective than one-on-one. When several people are sharing their ideas and thoughts, you naturally are introduced to a variety of ways of looking at something.

Tutoring takes a time commitment. In order for tutoring to be effective, you should receive it at least twice a week. This prevents too many things from piling up between sessions, and keeps what you covered in the previous session fresh in your mind. An advantage of having a tutor is that you don't necessarily have to work on a particular subject. You can be tutored in study strategies, for example, which will help your schoolwork across the board.

CLASSES

During the school year, your school may offer special courses on how to study. You also might benefit from taking summer school. Night school classes offered through continuing education programs and local community colleges also might interest you.

In recent years, many businesses have sprung up to help with academic subjects, such as reading and math, and to prepare students for special tests, such as the SAT® or the ACT. Look in the phone book for your area to see what is available near you. Ask teachers, counselors, and friends what programs they recommend.

STUDY GROUPS

If you have a problem, it's often a good idea to get help from someone in the same situation. If you are having problems studying, you can join or start a study group.

A study group is an excellent way to help yourself and others at the same time. Studying in a group offers a number of advantages. Group members offer one another support, guidance, and motivation. Studying with others helps you realize that other people have trouble too. Seeing this may make you less self-conscious about your own weaknesses. You may find yourself helping others in subjects that you understand well. Being able to help others makes anyone feel good. In addition, being an active member of a group can make you take your work more seriously. Knowing that others are counting on you can spur you to get the work done.

Members of a study group can offer different perspectives

on the same subject. Learning about something from different points of view helps you understand it better.

Set up some ground rules that help the group minimize or avoid conflict. For example, you may set rules saying that everyone has to listen without interrupting when someone speaks, everyone has to cooperate, everyone has to participate by speaking up, and everyone has to come prepared to work.

Your study group doesn't have to limit itself to studying from books alone. Find several sources of information and use as many as you can. You can visit museums. You can arrange

to meet with professionals and people who have firsthand experience of the topic you are studying. If you are studying a particular culture or country, you can prepare foods of that country or have a meal at a restaurant that serves them.

Another fun thing to do, for any topic, is to find books on it and share them with one another. Maybe you can make or build art projects. You can do science experiments or make topographic maps. You might even try videotaping a skit or acting out different characters from history or books. Make up games and brainteasers for each other. As a group, you can do many things that would be too complicated to tackle by yourself. For more tips on forming a study group, turn to chapters 8 and 10.

As you and your study group discuss what you're learning, lots of questions are going to arise. As you learn, it's as important to ask a question as it is to answer one. One expert, Norris Sanders, has classified seven different types of questions that make learning easier. They are: memory, translation, interpretation, application, logical analysis, synthesis, and evaluation. Each of these types is described in further detail on the following two pages.

Learn to make the question-and-answer process work for you and the other learners in your group. When you are studying, make sure to ask one another questions that go beyond memory and translation. The best questions are, of course, those that require creative thinking. Ask one another questions that lead to you to consider subjects in different ways and from various points of view. After all, the more questions you ask, the more you'll learn!

When you're studying alone, get in the habit of asking yourself questions *before* you begin your studies. That will help you determine which are the most important ideas and recognize relationships between ideas. You also can use the explanation of types of questions to analyze what a teacher is expecting when you turn in a particular assignment.

When you're reading, ask yourself questions to make sure you understand the information. After you've finished reading, ask yourself questions to make sure that you've absorbed the material properly and that you're ready to apply what you've learned.

Whether you decide to solve your study problems in a group or by working independently, remember that you are never alone. In this chapter, we've suggested a number of people to whom you can turn, from your parents to teachers and counselors. You also now have several strategies that you can use to overcome your difficulties.

YOU'RE NOT ALONE

When it comes to tackling a problem, that first step is often the hardest. Once you've taken it, though, chances are the rest will come a lot easier. Just don't be afraid to ask for help when you need it, and keep your spirits up by remaining positive about yourself and your abilities.

The seven types of questions are:

Memory—memory questions ask that you recognize or recall specific information. You don't have to explain anything to answer these questions.

Examples:

What is your name?

What is your address?

On what continent is the country of Ireland?

Translation—translation questions ask you to change the information into different form. You are not required to explain your answer.

Examples:

Summarize the events that lead to the fall of Rome.

Draw a picture of how a volcano erupts.

Diagram the water cycle.

Interpretation—interpretation questions ask you to make comparisons, determine cause and effect, and draw conclusions. You have to explain your answers to these questions.

Examples:

Compare and contrast football and rugby.

What would happen to the nutrients in soil if they weren't replenished?

Why is recycling important?

Application—application questions ask you to solve a real-life problem. To answer these types of questions, you have to use what you know from experience.

Examples:

How can you help solve the problem of pollution?

How would you improve profits if you owned a grocery store?

How would you design a safer skateboard?

Logical analysis—logical analysis questions ask you to analyze and evaluate the logic of an idea. You have to make a strong argument for or against the question. The reasons you give are more important than the stand that you take.

Examples:

Is violence ever a solution to a problem?

Does Socialism create a more equal society?

Is *Charlotte's Web* the best title for this book?

Synthesis—synthesis questions ask you to suggest creative solutions to a problem. To answer these questions, you have to come up with original ideas.

Examples:

If you were President, what would you do about the national deficit?

What changes can this country make in order to spend money on health care more wisely?

In what way could the testing of high school students be made more fair?

Evaluation—evaluation questions ask you to judge something against a set of standards. You have to explain what you think and why.

Examples:

Is *The New York Times* a good newspaper?

Is granola good for you?

Did the *Stars & Stripes* deserve to win the America's Cup in 1988?

Wherever you turn for help, you'll be glad you did! By learning how to meet these challenges head on, you'll be positioning yourself for greater success later on in life. Everyone—teen-agers and adults, students and teachers—faces problems every day. The winners aren't people who are free of worries. That's impossible. The winners are those who use their resources to overcome problems.

APPENDIX:
LEARNING IN THE HOME

As parents, you want to help your children set and reach goals. You want them to be successful and feel successful. In previous chapters, we discussed a variety of ways to make studying lead to learning. Just as you and your children need to be aware of learning strategies, you need to know how to choose the ones that are best for your younger children. In the same way, you can encourage activities that build your children's character. Qualities of good character, such as responsibility, independence, perseverance, ability to manage time, and self-reliance, go beyond the classroom and what's taught there. They prepare your children for learning and for life. It is important to teach these qualities before your children go to school and nurture them once they start school.

Responsibility

To be responsible is to be trustworthy and accountable for one's actions, to know right from wrong, and to be able to think and act reasonably. As your children grow, you and their teachers expect them to take on ever greater responsibilities. Children themselves expect to do so as well.

Once your children know how to dress themselves, prepare their own breakfast, and make their beds, those tasks become their responsibility. As a parent, you may be quite ready for your child to accept those responsibilities. But responsibilities involving judgment—such as making friends, deciding how to spend free time, and choosing how to behave in public—may be more difficult for you to pass on to your children. After all, responsibilities that require judgment are more complicated. Because you can see the far-reaching consequences of actions better than your children can, you may be reluctant to let them make their own decisions. You may be tempted to sit with your children as they do their homework to help them avoid mistakes. But if you do that, how will your child learn to assume the responsibilities of school, and later the workplace?

The responsibility for getting homework done on time belongs with your children. By shouldering their responsibility as students, they will begin to do so in other areas of their lives. To encourage this, ask them when they plan to do something instead of telling them when to do it. If they tell you that they are going to do their homework 15 minutes before bedtime, ask if they think they'll be able to do their best work at that time. Help your child decide to rethink this. He or she will be more willing to work within self-imposed guidelines rather than ones you have imposed.

If your children are not yet in school, put them in charge of a particular chore. It can be anything: keeping their toys and room tidy, putting away their laundry, sweeping, helping make up the grocery list, and so on. Let your children know you are proud of the good job they are doing and how important their help is to the family.

Independence

Independence is the capacity to act on ones's own, to decide what needs to be done and how. Your children first showed their independence when they started saying "no" to you. They told you in no uncertain terms that they weren't going to wear a certain outfit or eat broccoli or take naps anymore.

However, you may fear your children's independence as they grow older. You may feel comfortable letting your children decide when to clean their rooms, but when it comes to their health, safety, or happiness, you probably want to hold onto control a bit longer. That's understandable. In no way should you let your children's quest for independence put them in danger. However, if you don't let them spread their wings, they'll never fly. You cannot always be there for them. They need to find the strength within themselves to stand up to challenges and face life head-on.

Working on homework without assistance is a very safe way for children to test their independence. If you help too much, your children will not realize they can do things themselves. With a few well-chosen questions, you can help your children solve homework problems: "What do you think would happen if. . .?" "Why are you doing it that way?" "What other ways have you tried to solve this problem?" By asking instead of directing, you will honor your children's independence. And you will probably be amazed at what they tell you!

Giving younger children choices provides them with opportunities to exert their independence. Ask, "Would you rather have grilled cheese or peanut butter for lunch?" Or, "Would you rather paint pictures this afternoon or go to the library?" Show them that you take their wishes seriously, by listening to their suggestions and acting on them.

Perseverance

Infants often seem to be the most persistent human beings on earth. When they want something, they do whatever it takes to get it. Their perseverance not only gets others to respond to their need for food or attention, but also helps them develop the skill and coordination to do things on their own. When babies physically are ready to turn over, stand, crawl, or walk, they don't give up until they can do it.

Perseverance requires that your children try and try again, even if they fail the first, second, or even the hundredth time. Each time they try, they get a little closer to the mark until at last—sometimes at long last—they reach their goal. Sometimes, your children become frustrated. This frustration is a call for help, not a call for rescuing. Whenever you see your children becoming frustrated, give them a chance to figure out the solution. Letting them work things out on their own will develop their stamina for perseverance.

You can teach perseverance by not letting your children give up when faced with a challenge—whether it's homework, a social situation, or a personal project. This doesn't mean pushing them relentlessly; it means offering them support and encouragement and the belief that they can do whatever they have set out to do if they really try. Remind them that progress is often slower than they would like, but even though they might feel stuck, they are still getting somewhere. Once they see that perseverance leads to progress, they will learn to be patient as they stick with a task.

Letting younger children solve puzzles, build with blocks, and perform simple science experiments will build perseverance. Allow your children plenty of time to work things out on their own, and encourage them to tell you about the process. It takes a great amount of perseverance to participate in sports. So expose them to activities that require skill, such as swimming, gymnastics, and even playing catch.

PRESCHOOLERS

Managing time

Throughout their lives, your children will need to know how to manage their time. The number of hours in a day, days in a week, and weeks in a year are the same for everyone. But some people seem to get more done than others. You probably would like to see your children work hard and play hard. But unless they know how to manage their time, they'll hardly find enough for either, let alone both.

By helping your children decide when to study, play, exercise, and relax, you can help them develop a healthy lifestyle. You know the time of day when your children are at their best. By teaching them to do certain activities at the best time, you make children feel better about themselves. Children may not understand that if they ignore their homework until they're almost ready for bed, they will be too tired to concentrate. But no natural law says that homework has to be done in the evening. If your children are morning people, encourage them to get up early to do their homework.

SCHOOL-AGED CHILDREN

Managing time also means setting up schedules for individual projects. Getting homework done on time means planning for long and short assignments. By discussing with your children what worked well in the past and what didn't, they'll begin to see what they should try in the future and what they should avoid. Help your children set up a schedule, and encourage them to stick to it.

Try posting weekly schedules of all family members. This gives your children an example of what you're trying to teach them. The schedules will show where other family members are and when they'll be returning home. You can easily help children draw up realistic schedules simply by asking questions: "How much time are you allowing yourself?" "Did you leave enough time to get there?" "How much time did it take the last time?"

Younger children may have little perception of time, but you can help them become more aware of it. For example, try giving youngsters some warning when you want them to move from one activity to the next. Before going on to something new, say, "In 15 minutes you're going to have to put that game away because it will be time for lunch." Then, remind them every five minutes so that they are prepared when it's time to put the game away.

You can help children plan their time by letting them know what the day holds. Suppose they want to go to the beach, but you don't have enough time. Explain the problem as simply as you can. Change your plans for the day or set a date to go to the beach in the near future. This can help your children understand how to fit activities into the day or postpone them until a better time. Give your children choices. Tell them, "If you want to go to the park, we won't have time to go to the library. Which would you rather do today?"

Initiative

Think of all the times when initiative will help your children. They need initiative to begin anything on their own, whether it is amusing themselves or doing their homework. Whose ideas are your children more open to, yours or theirs? Have you ever given your children a list of chores that they ignored? Or a list of fun things to do that they yawned at? Children prefer doing things they want to do, when they want to do them. Sometimes, however, chores or homework need to be done whether your children "feel" like doing them or not. How do you encourage your children to take initiative in doing things that are good for them?

Children are quite capable of seeing that something needs to be done, deciding when to do it, and proceeding to do so. Help your children take initiative by telling them what needs to be done and letting them choose the time. If you encourage your children to be self-starters rather than imposing all kinds of rules, you can prevent arguments about what needs to be done and when. The more choices your children make about when to do what, the better they'll become at making those decisions.

Naturally, you want to save your children the frustration and disappointment that can come with lack of initiative. You may want to prod and cajole them into taking on new activities. But unless it is a life-or-death situation, don't force them do things before they get the urge. They'll show more enthusiasm for tasks they choose than those you choose for them.

Allowing your children to take initiative with their home-work is a safe way to let them practice and develop this quali-ty. Some well-intentioned questions can help: "How are you going to begin?" "What's your next step?" "Do you have a back-up plan in case that doesn't work?" "What is it?"

SCHOOL-AGED CHILDREN

You can develop initiative in younger children by giving them a choice of things to do. Make the activities relatively diverse, for example, reading; writing; painting; or playing a pretend game. Encourage your children to make up a play and put it on for you. Letting your children decide how to fill their own time helps them develop initiative—and gives you more free time.

PRESCHOOLERS

Self-reliance

Children need to learn to rely on themselves, to trust their per-sonal abilities and judgment. In order to make good decisions throughout their lives, they need plenty of practice. Children who are confident and have high self-esteem believe in them-selves. They can face peer pressure, see the difference be-tween right and wrong, and act accordingly. Children who never have to rely on themselves, by contrast, may doubt their ability to make good decisions.

If you encourage your children to do their homework them-selves, they'll need to search for the answers to their own problems. Letting your children be self-reliant—even when you know a faster, better, or easier way—is a gift to them. They'll find the faster, better, easier way soon enough on their own. Support your children's self-reliance by not offering your own opinions, and asking instead, "What did you do last time?" "Is that something you'd do again?" "What would you

SCHOOL-AGED CHILDREN

change to make your plan better?" "Where have you looked for the solution?" "Where else might you look?"

One way to develop self-reliance in younger children is by encouraging them to find their own lost possessions. Give them plenty of hints, but let them have the satisfaction of finding them on their own. Show your children that they can trust themselves, and let them participate as much as possible in taking care of themselves. Let them help prepare their own meals; pick out their own outfits (no matter how they clash); wrap presents; and write their own cards, even if it's just a line or a scribble. Anything that gives your children a sense that they're capable of doing something will encourage self-reliance.

Showing the way

What can you do to encourage and develop these qualities in your children? One way is to set a good example. As discussed in Chapter 1, your children learn behavior, ways of thinking, and values from your actions.

Another powerful factor is trust. If you trust your children to do something and to give it their best, that is exactly what they will do. People live up or down to others' expectations of them. If you urge your children to think and act independently, they will become increasingly better at making decisions.

Remember when your children were babies and you child-proofed your home? You didn't turn off the electricity or throw away all your cleaning products. Instead, you put plugs in unused outlets, safety locks on cabinets, and your treasures beyond reach. You did this so that your children would have freedom to explore without you constantly saying "no" or "don't touch" or "be careful." You wanted to make your home safe, and you wanted to enjoy your children instead of being a safety monitor.

You can do the same for your children as they grow, mentally and emotionally. To see your children explore ideas and their abilities, encourage and support their independence. When they persevere, let them know that you respect that. Don't demand instant results. Take their questions seriously, but try not to be the only source of information. If you'd like to be a part of your children's education, it is more helpful to take an active interest than to supply all the answers. Go to the library with them. Read some of the books they bring home so that you can discuss the ideas inside.

Find out what your children know and how they understand by asking them questions. Don't limit yourself to questions that may be on a test. Ask them why they think as they do. For example, instead of asking your children who was the first President of the United States, ask them why they think George Washington was chosen to be the President.

Ask younger children why they said or did something, or why they enjoyed a particular activity or story. Encourage children to explain their opinions. If your children ask you a question, ask them what they think before you answer. By getting your children to talk, you can find out a lot about how they think.

When they answer the question, "What do you think?" your children may find that they know more than they realized. That realization will spur them to find the rest of the information they need. Ask your children "why?" or "why not?" often. As your children answer, they get a firmer grasp of ideas and become more aware of how and what they think.

Take the time simply to be with your children, whether you take a walk around the block, go to the museum, or read a book together. If you make yourself available to your children, you'll show them they are important enough to spend time with. Let them see that you're interested in them, not only as children, but as people who have ideas, thoughts, and experiences to share with you.

SPEND SOME TIME

Taking time just to "be" gives you and your children an opportunity to talk and listen to one another. In today's world, many people feel pulled in different directions. Sometimes it's hard to relax and pay attention to your child when you're trying to get dinner on the table or you're rushing to the dry cleaner before it closes. But your children will learn to value themselves only if you value them. They will reward your trust when you give it. And for them to talk openly to you, you must be open yourself.

Use the power of encouragement in all aspects of your children's lives. Let them know that you see them working to figure things out, that you see them taking time to learn something. Focus on what your children are doing right. Honest praise is an amazing motivator. It's the way to make your children aware that they can succeed. By focusing on what your children can do, you give them the courage to do more and to put their hearts into it. Children's beliefs about themselves, their lovableness, and their abilities are based on your belief in them.

Activities for learning

Many of the everyday things you do with your children prepare them to succeed in school. Here is a list of activities that children age 3 and up can enjoy. Tailor the activities to your children's skills. Remember, children who can scribble consider themselves writers and children who tell stories as they turn the pages in a picture book consider themselves readers. Encourage these beliefs. Give correct spellings or pronuncia-

Provide your children with:
- Plenty of paper for all kinds for writing and art projects: colored construction paper, graph paper, lined paper, unlined paper, rolls of adding machine paper, rolls of kraft paper, or butcher paper
- Materials to write, draw, or paint with: pencils, pens, colored markers (narrow and broad tipped), crayons, calligraphy pens and ink or felt-tipped calligraphy pens, tempera paints, water colors, paint brushes, and colored pencils
- Supplies such as glue, erasers, pencil sharpeners, staples, staplers, paper clips, rubber bands, yarn, and scissors
- Art materials, such as clay, papier mâché, scraps of wood, cardboard, yarn, and string
- Found objects, such as rocks, sticks, leaves, pine cones, pods, seeds, and flowers
- Old newspapers, magazines, and junk mail for projects and pictures
- Sewing supplies, such as needles, thread, yarn, embroidery thread, and scraps of material
- Puzzles
- Blocks and other building materials

tions for words only if your children ask. And stop at that. Don't explain how letters sound. Your children only want the word so that they can continue writing or reading. If you give them more than they ask for, you could break their concentration and destroy their interest. Let them tell you what they want from you.

On page 208 is a list of materials that can help your children play creatively. Take your children's ages into account. Keep small, pointed, or sharp objects out of the reach of toddlers. Teach older children the safe way to use potentially dangerous items, such as scissors.

Your children will find many ways to create things with these materials. Encourage them to make particular items, and to experiment freely. By giving your children fun ways to use their heads and their hands, you will be developing small motor coordination as well as mental ability.

Your children also need to develop their gross motor coordination. To do this, get them involved in physical activities, such as dancing, playing sports, running, cycling, and gymnastics.

You don't have to be a historian to give your children a

You can do many things to make learning fun for your children. Here are some suggestions.

- Play and make music
- Read books and tell stories
- Expose them to poetry and songs, and word games such as jokes, riddles, and puns; teach them rhymes and chants, and make up your own
- Go to concerts and plays and museums
- Share your family history through storytelling, photo albums, and visits with relatives
- Give your children chores, such as helping with cooking or gardening to involve them in family life

---

sense of history. Nor do you have to be an artist, musician, or scientist to give your children a love of these disciplines. Your children will remain curious and eager to learn—if you open the world to them and give them a taste of everything.

RESOURCES

Glossary

Analytic thinking: Synthesizing information by breaking it down into parts. Analytic thinking involves acting logically, following directions, and putting thoughts into words.

Clustering: A study tool in which a student groups related topics together for better understanding.

Compulsivity: The degree to which a student performs unnecessary tasks while studying, such as copying notes before studying them, thereby wasting time.

Computer-aided instruction: Software that teaches a variety of subjects. The computer takes the student through a lesson step by step and contains a built-in evaluation system.

Cubing: A method of gathering thoughts by listing questions and answers on a cube.

Distractibility: The degree to which a student's concentration is broken by external and internal factors.

Global thinking: Synthesizing information by making parts into a whole. Global thinking involves intuition, subjective thinking, and daydreaming.

Graphic organizer: A study device that helps illustrate, organize, and simplify information to aid understanding.

Imaging: Forming mental pictures while reading.

INSERT: A method of active reading in which the reader marks the material to reflect the reader's response.

Learning environment: The student's workspace. It includes sound, lighting, temperature, and visual distractions.

Paired summarizing: A method of study in which two partners take turns summarizing and discussing information.

Look-back: Reviewing what was read already.

Motivation: What causes a person to do something or act in a certain way or creates enjoyment from a task.

PReP: A pre-reading plan in which a student follows a series of steps that encourages active reading. The student asks, "What do I think?" and "Why do I think that?" and then revises original ideas based on new information.

ReQuest: Reciprocal questioning. A method of study in which two partners take turns answering and asking questions.

Paired questioning: A method of study that combines *paired reading* and *reciprocal questioning*.

Paired reading: A method of study whereby each person takes turns listening and recalling the information.

Paraphrasing: Putting what you read into your own words.

REAP: A method of study that involves reading, encoding, annotating, and pondering.

Outlining: In taking notes, writing only the main features or leading characteristics of any subject.

Synthesize: To form ideas by bringing together separate pieces of information.

Visualization: A way to solve problems mentally. With visualization, the student pictures himself or herself solving the problem, step by step.

For further reading

Borger, Robert, and Seaborne, A. E. *The Psychology of Learning.* 2nd ed. Penguin, 1982.

Carey, Helen H., and Judith E. Greenberg. *How to Use Your Community as a Resource.* Watts, 1983. Grades 7-9.

Cohen, Daniel. *Intelligence: What Is It?* Evans & Co., 1974. Grades 5-8.

Edson, Lee. *How We Learn.* Time-Life Books, 1975.

Fischler, Martin A., and Firshein, Oscar. *Intelligence: The Eye, the Brain, and the Computer.* Addison-Wesley, 1987.

Gall, Meredith D., and Gall, J. P. *Making the Grade: Raising Your GPA by Studying Smarter, Not Harder.* 2nd rev. ed. Prima Pub., 1992.

Gallant, Roy A. *Memory: How It Works and How to Improve It.* Macmillan, 1984. First published in 1980. Grades 5-8.

Hawes, Gene R., and Lynne Salop Hawes. *Hawes Guide to Successful Study Skills.* NAL, 1991. Grades 9-12.

Healy, Jane M. *Your Child's Growing Mind: A Parent's Guide to Learning from Birth to Adolescence.* Doubleday, 1987.

James, Elizabeth, and Carol Barkin. *School Smarts: How to Succeed at Schoolwork.* Lothrop Lee & Shepard Books, 1988. Grades 5-8.

Klavan, Ellen. *Taming the Homework Monster: How to Make Homework a Positive Learning Experience for Your Child.* Poseidon, 1987

Lorayne, Harry. *How to Develop a Super-Power Memory.* NAL, 1974. Grades 10-12.

Schneider, Zola Dincin, and Phyllis B. Kalb. *Countdown to College: A Student's Guide to Getting the Most Out of High School.* College Entrance Examination Board, 1989.

Tchudi, Stephen. *The Young Learner's Handbook.* Macmillan, 1987. Grades 6-9.

INDEX